W9-AAK-844

PARADIGM

LOST

<rediscovering God's plan for spiritual harvest

Paradigm Lost

Rediscovering God's Plan for Spiritual Harvest

Dr. Howard Foltz

and

Ruth Ford

Authentic
MEDIA

Authentic Media
We welcome your comments and questions.
129 Mobilization Drive, Waynesboro, GA 30830 USA authenticusa@stl.org

and 9 Holdom Avenue, Bletchley, Milton Keynes, Bucks, MK1 1QR, UK
www.authenticbooks.com

If you would like a copy of our current catalog, contact us at:
1-8MORE-BOOKS
ordersusa@stl.org

Paradigm Lost
ISBN: 1-932805-05-2

Copyright © 2004 by Dr. Howard Foltz and Ruth Ford

09 08 07 06 05   6 5 4 3 2 1
First published in 2005 by Authentic Media

All rights reserved. No part of this book may be reproduced in any form
without permission in writing from the publisher, except in the case of brief
quotations embodied in critical articles or reviews.

All scripture quotations, unless otherwise indicated, are taken from the HOLY
BIBLE, NEW INTERNATIONAL VERSION®. NIV®. Copyright ©1973,
1978, 1984 by International Bible Society. Used by permission of Zondervan.
All rights reserved.

Library of Congress Cataloging-in-Publication Data

Foltz, Howard L., 1939-
  Paradigm lost : rediscovering God's plan for spiritual harvest / Howard Foltz, Ruth Ford.
    p. cm.
  Includes bibliographical references.
  ISBN 1-932805-05-2 (pbk.)
  1. Missions. I. Ford, Ruth, 1963- II. Title.

  BV2061.3.F65 2005
  266--dc22

                          2005000975

Cover design: Paul Lewis
Interior design: Angela Duerksen
Editorial team: Karen James, Tom Richards, and Betsy Weinrich

Printed in the United States of America

Contents

P A R A

∠ acknowledgements

A project like this is never the result of labor from just two people. It requires support from understanding spouses and ministry partners. It also requires an environment that encourages curiosity and allows legitimate questions to take root and grow into legitimate answers. And it requires a host of people who are willing to lend their expertise in areas where we lack knowledge, wisdom, and understanding.

Many such people deserve to be acknowledged and thanked for their investment of time and experience in helping us write this book.

We are grateful to Pat Foltz and Bill Ford, our spouses, for the multitude of ways they undergirded this effort.

We thank Regent University and Accelerating International Mission Strategies (AIMS) for providing the time and the opportunity to explore the agricultural paradigm as it applies to spiritual harvest.

We acknowledge the pastors and church leaders who responded to our questionnaire and who agreed to be interviewed for the purpose of gaining and clarifying information. We also note that Dr. Foltz has spoken in churches around the world for forty-one years. He estimates that he has ministered to perhaps thousands of congregations in that time, and they have contributed to the rich experience that gave birth to this book.

We are grateful to Ray Hollowell for lending us his expertise in both farming and local church ministry. We thank

Dr. Chreston Holoman, who helped us understand various points of Hebraic tradition including the Biblical feasts.

We also want to express appreciation to Chris Jones for his help in putting together the list of resources for people who want to invest some time in researching a specific culture. We thank Johanne Jean-Jacques, Margaret Reitz, Martha Underwood, Pat West, and Bob Williams, who helped with researching and proofreading this manuscript. And we thank the members of the AIMS staff and of the Sunday night LIFE group at Emmaus Church in Chesapeake, Virginia, for consistently praying for the progress and success of this project.

We are grateful to Volney James, publisher at Authentic Media, and to Angela Duerksen, editorial manager, for their confidence and partnership in our work, and to Karen James, the editor who helped us wind our way through the maze of final details related to the completion of this book. And we recognize the efforts of our proofreaders, Tom Richards and Betsy Weinrich.

Most important, we thank God for the privilege of serving with him in this world's harvest fields. We pray this book will be instrumental in raising up a new generation of harvesters of every generation and on every continent.

≥ foreword

Y ou can take the boy out of the farm, but you can't take the farm out of the boy. I know, because I was raised by a farmer and veterinarian in Indiana. My mornings, afternoons, and weekends throughout my childhood were spent toiling with feed, hay, and farm tools. To this day, it's not hard for me to wake up early when there's work to be done, because when I was a boy the day began when the sun broke through the windows. It's not hard for me to wait for results, because I understand that the seasons do their work slowly. And it's not hard for me to comprehend the agricultural context of mission work in the Bible, because there's no better symbol for what happens in the human heart than the sowing and reaping that takes place on the plains of the Midwest every year.

I've always believed that the best life principles can be gleaned from nature, which is why I've never tried to get the farm out of me. In fact, though my family now lives just outside a city, for most of my kids' lives we've had farm animals. My four boys and my daughter know how to ride horses and clean chicken coops. They know how to tend grass and deal with weeds. And through spending so many Saturday mornings doing those very things, they know a lot about how to live.

Now, though I love my childhood and have a deep appreciation for God's creation, I'm not at all adverse to advances in technology. I believe we're living in a generation of opportunity. We have a phenomenal chance to fulfill the Great Commission precisely because the Lord has given us some technological tools that are helping us get His work done. I could write this foreword on an airplane on my way to a conference in Kiev, Ukraine, email it to my editor in Boston, Massachusetts, and have him send it to my office in Colorado Springs, Colorado. Once the book is written and edited, the publisher could have the files typeset, printed, bound, and sent to the warehouse and this valuable information could be spreading around the world in a matter of weeks. That's progress, and it blesses the kingdom of God. It brings us closer together, helping us all to receive and benefit from Dr. Foltz's ideas and apply them to our lives.

But as Dr. Foltz makes clear, there are dangers inherent to all of our technological progress, and we've all noted those dangers before. There's far too much noise in our culture. There's far too little rest. There's too much emphasis on speed and not enough on quality. Too much focus on accomplishment, too little on relationship.

At its worst, our fast-paced, techno-centric culture causes us to misread God's word and to miss out on fantastic, life-giving principles just because we don't have the eyes to see them. We've moved so far from an agriculturally based, land-conscious, deep-rooted society that many of the biblical references to farming and nature seem foreign to modern ears.

Which is precisely why we need books like this one. With tenderness, compassion, and grace, Dr. Foltz eases us back toward the agricultural paradigm of the Bible. He points us toward a mentality that takes into account the principles that God built into His creation. He reminds us of the importance of seasons, the significance of the created elements, and the divinity of time. And, most importantly, Dr. Foltz explains what all this has to do with knowing Christ and spreading the gospel.

It's that last thing—spreading the gospel—that really fuels this book. Dr. Foltz is not just celebrating the land. He's telling us why God communicates the way He does, and showing us what it all has to do with God's larger purposes. Dr. Foltz is a farmer, planting seeds of truth and love, and he's also a harvester, reaping people for the kingdom of God.

One of my favorite things about this book is how much it is focused on the local church. Dr. Foltz takes Jesus' call to minister locally *and* abroad—"in Jerusalem, throughout Judea, in Samaria, and to the ends of the earth"—and applies it to every local church-based congregation of believers. I love that idea, and I think the best churches around the world are the ones that are practicing it.

I also love the breadth of this book—Dr. Foltz manages to say a little bit about everything! In a sense, *Paradigm Lost* is really a book about general life principles: how to have goals, create a mission statement, persevere, rest, be steady in all circumstances, and more. Every observation has an application. Dr. Foltz does not just offer us abstract exegesis of the agricultural context of Scripture; he explains how we can apply it to our lives, our churches, and to the ongoing mission of the body of Christ worldwide.

So, sit down in a big chair, take off your watch, turn off your cell phone, and let Dr. Foltz guide you into the fields. He'll challenge your thinking a little bit, turn your head around, and help you regain a biblical paradigm for doing the work of God.

Ted Haggard

P A R A

∠ introduction

My co-writer, Ruth Ford, claims to be directionally challenged. In fact, she told me that in college she lived in a dorm that was built like a maze to cut down on noise. For the first two weeks of every year, she consistently got lost trying to find her room.

In that way, she's like my wife Pat. Once when we lived in Germany and she was driving, I told her, "Honey, when they start speaking French, turn around and go back."

We have all been in situations where we needed a good map. Clearly, when it comes to spiritual issues, Scripture is the best map of all. The Bible defines where we are, it tells us where we should be, and it helps us know how to get from "here" to "there."

But just having a really good map does not guarantee that the person who owns it also knows how to read it. Even a mapping professional can lack the tools that help him or her interpret a map accurately. Ruth's father-in-law worked for years as a cartographer, analyzing geographic information and creating maps. Because of his expertise, the family acquiesced to his opinions as to which routes they should take on a recent vacation. But when he looked at a map, he always wore his glasses. They helped him see clearly, so he could correctly interpret the symbols and apply the information in a practical way. This book grew from the understanding that Scripture is the "map" for every aspect of personal life and public ministry and, specifically, for kingdom growth. But we cannot adequately understand the map if we are not wearing the right glasses. In no way is this book a substitute for the Bible. Nor is it a run-of-the-mill "how-to" manual for church development. It goes deeper than the quick fix. It is not so much focused on giving new information about evangelism or missions. Rather, it is focused on restoring the biblical lenses through which we interpret and apply that information.

I want to change the way we *see* and *think about* church—which naturally will change the way we *do* church.

After two years of research and writing, re-researching and re-writing, I believe this book is a prophetic call to God's people to return to *his* plan for world evangelization. In short, this book calls Christians to restore a harvest mentality to the local church. Why is that important? Jesus primarily used agricultural language to describe his plan. He chose that language, not simply because he was speaking to farmers, but because the agricultural metaphors best fit the process he had in mind.

This book is not intended to imply that people who do not have an agrarian mindset cannot be successful in ministry. It simply puts forth the ideal that growing God's kingdom will happen most naturally if we subscribe to the agrarian view that supports scriptural language related to this issue.

Chapter one describes how Western culture has moved away from the agrarian view and how the Western church has mirrored that shift. It explains the negative ramifications and builds a case for the restoration of an agrarian mindset as it relates to the priority of growing God's kingdom. Chapters two through five explain the biblical root of the harvest mindset, and chapters six through thirteen describe the practical fruit of the harvest mindset. This book certainly is not the last word on spiritual harvest, but it is designed to spark discussion and dialogue related to this crucial topic.

God's Kingdom Is Global

Almost two decades ago, God led and helped me to found a ministry now called Accelerating International Mission Strategies (AIMS). As its name implies, this organization exists to hasten the rate at which God's people are sowing and reaping the seeds of his kingdom all over the world. Specifically, our mission is to "challenge the Church to take the gospel where it has never been proclaimed." We serve as an advocate for the half of the world's population that has never had a legitimate opportunity to respond to the gospel. They may never have heard the good news of salvation; or they may have heard it delivered in a way they could not understand.

While we are not oblivious to the importance of nurturing the "crop" of people who already populate our churches, we teach believers to look to new fields near them—people who need to be evangelized in their own community and in similar cultures—and then to look further, to those fields that have never been adequately prepared, where the seed of the gospel has never been adequately invested. AIMS is based on the ideal that every local church in the world has a mandate to minister in its own body, in its own community and culture, in similar cultures, and in entirely unfamiliar cultures.

The Bible's harvest mandate clearly has a global focus. Missions consultant Tom Telford recalls an essay turned in by a student at Columbia International University. She wrote, "My Bible oozes with missions." She added, "I think I must have a special Bible because other people don't seem to think their Bibles ooze. Or maybe it's because my Bible has transformed itself over the years, because, now that I think about it, my Bible seems to talk a lot more about missions now than it did five years ago."[1]

She concluded, of course, that her Bible hadn't changed—she had. She understood that God's desire for relationship is not limited to any one culture or ethnic group. He wants to see his kingdom stretch across the whole world. So, while this is not intended to be specifically a missions book, it supports the ideal of cross-cultural ministry for every local church.

The Ideal of Closure

This book also is based on a specific goal. Missions strategists call it closure. Simply put, that means God calls people to the specific and strategic task of completing the Great Commission. This was Jesus' final mandate before he returned to heaven: "All authority in heaven and on earth has been given to me. Therefore go and make disciples of all nations, baptizing them in the name of the Father and of the Son and of the Holy Spirit, and teaching them to obey everything I have commanded you. And surely I am with you always, to the very end of the age" (Matthew 28:18–20). (See parallel accounts in Mark 16, Luke 24, and Acts 1.)

We at AIMS do not see local evangelism and global missions as an "either/or" proposition. We see it as a "both/and." God is interested in spiritual harvest in your neighborhood. He also is interested in harvest among the Tuareg people of West Africa, or the Turkic people of Eurasia, or the Sundanese people of Indonesia, and the list could go on and on.

We believe God has given his people the responsibility to establish true, biblically based, culturally relevant churches in every people group on earth—and not just to plant churches, but to establish church planting movements. Harvest is not an end in itself; it always has the long-term goal of producing another harvest. That means we must develop churches that can and will reproduce themselves. The global mandate extends to them as well. They should be involved in ministry to one another, but also in outreach to their own culture, similar cultures, and entirely different cultures. When we have partnered with God in his plan and have successfully planted those kinds of movements in every culture on earth, we will have brought closure to the Great Commission. So join us as we return to a better understanding of Jesus' intention when he used agricultural terminology to describe the process that will accomplish that task.

A "P.S." from the co-writer

This book has been an adventure. When I agreed to work on this project, I thought it would be relatively easy. I was a country girl from a missionary family. Because the underlying theme married those two experiences, I thought this book was tailor-made for me. I didn't expect to read so much about tractor development and farm implements and soil erosion and various types of seeds and plants. I also didn't know the spiritual applications would challenge me to realign my own preconceived ministry ideals with Scripture. I had no idea I would have to wrestle through my own "paradigm shift," recommitting myself to the harvest principles carefully laid out in this book.

This book is the result of reading and prayer, research and prayer, interviews and prayer, pondering and prayer, writing and prayer. . . . So please, pray as you read it. It's not the final word on spiritual harvest, but we hope it will help you clean and maybe even restore your biblical glasses as you re-read

P   A   R   A

Scripture in a new light. God has challenged and blessed me through the writing. I pray he will also challenge and bless you through the reading.

chapter 1 < paradigm lost

A s a rookie umpire for major league baseball, Durwood Merrill faced the challenge of calling strikes for fastball pitcher Nolan Ryan. Merrill handled the first pitch fine. Then . . . FWUMP! The catcher's mitt swallowed the second pitch. Merrill hesitated. He deliberated. He called it a strike. Ryan's opponent leaned backwards; stepping outside the batter's box, he reassured the newcomer. "Ump, don't feel bad," he said. "I didn't see it either."[1]

Many of us, out of breath from the rapid pace of recent history, feel like Merrill. We didn't see the changes coming. We're not sure how they got here, but still we have to deal with them. Technology has opened new opportunities, simplifying many aspects of life, but also altering our pace. Our banks have drive-thru windows and ATMs. Our offices have fax machines, pagers, cell phones, e-mail, and instant messaging. We are a society of technocrats, communicating with abbreviations because we don't have time to say (or type) the whole term. We're more likely to e-mail a joke to our neighbors than to tell it over the back fence. When they reply with an LOL (laugh out loud), we won't really know if they even cracked a smile. We pepper conversations with words like RAM and VR. When we say "web," we don't mean Charlotte's. When we say "megabyte," we don't mean a big snack. And when we say "terminal," we aren't referring to an illness.

Technology has made us impatient. We live in a minute-rice and instant-potato world. "Slow cookers" exist only for convenience. We plug them in so our meals will be ready when we return home, commuting through hurry-up traffic, from information-laden jobs, so we can get caught up on tasks left un-done during the day.

The Information Age

Western culture tries to sip information from a fire hose till we are drowning in data. Filmmakers and authors Peter and Paul Lalonde cite statistics indicating that the total amount of human knowledge doubled between 4000 BC and the birth of Christ. It doubled again between A.D. 1 and 1750. Then again, between 1750 and 1900. Again between 1900 and 1950. Again between 1950 and 1960. Now the total amount of human knowledge doubles every two years. The Lalondes explain, "We now know twice as much as we did just two short years ago, and half as much as we will know two years down the road." In fact, they tell us that "if you read just one full issue of the *New York Times* newspaper, you will have absorbed more information than you would have in your entire lifetime had you been born a hundred years ago."[2]

Computers fuel this information explosion. In 1972, only about 150 thousand computers existed in the entire world. By the year 2000, according to the U.S. Census Bureau, in the U.S. alone, 54 million households had one or more computers. That's 51 percent of all households, up from 42 percent just two years previously. The Census Bureau also indicates that, of the total U.S. adult population, almost one-third used e-mail from home, and about one-eighth of all adults surveyed used Internet connections in their homes to perform tasks related to their jobs.[3] And that was in 2000. Computers are so necessary, it's hard to imagine life without them.

We've Lost Our Roots

Technology was supposed to make our lives easier, and in many ways, it has. But it also has stolen some essential aspects of our culture and history. We've literally lost our roots. Statistics vary—some say 2 percent of the U.S. population is still involved in food production. Others say it is as high as 4 percent. It's a minor variance. The point is most of our population is ignorant of the hard work and specialized knowledge that puts food on our tables and clothes on our backs.

As theologian and author Leonard Sweet explained, "In the 'olden' days when I was born, my generation had at least one set of grandparents who were still tied to the farm in some way, giving us memories of farm living. In the 2000 census, they aren't even counting farmers because there are so few of them (under 2 million, with anticipations of only 600 thousand farmers left by the year 2020.) Average age of farmers today? Sixty."[4]

These statistics are mirrored in other Western countries as well. France, for instance, is the leading agricultural producer in the European Union, accounting for 23 percent of the region's agricultural production. Farmland still covers just over half of France's countryside. But in the twelve years between 1988 and 2000, more than a third of this nation's farms disappeared. Estimates in 2002 revealed "farmers and their dependents account for just 3.5 percent of the population, down from 12 percent in 1970."[5]

Similarly, the National Farmers Union, representing farmers in England and Wales, notes that farming employs less than 2 percent of the UK workforce. Most UK farmers fall into the forty-five to fifty-four age group, "with no sign of an influx of youngsters in the industry."[6]

These kinds of statistics imply that most Westerners no longer get their hands dirty. We may garden to beautify our yards and supplement our menus, but our survival does not depend on our personal involvement in harvest. Most Western children think milk comes from the refrigerator section at the local grocery store. They might recognize corn, but they couldn't tell wheat from oats if they saw an "amber field of grain." They've never faced the reality that an animal died to provide last night's hamburgers.

Lest you think I exaggerate, Ruth, my co-writer, recalls tutoring two elementary-aged children in an inner-city environment. They were reading *The Boy Who Cried Wolf*, a fable about a shepherd who yelled that a wolf was attacking the sheep. After reading the story, Ruth questioned the girls to gauge their comprehension. She found neither of them knew what a sheep was. They had never seen one. In fact, they had never seen even a picture of one.

Technology has reshaped our lives in many ways. Yet, this loss of our link with the land may be among the most profound. We have learned to think in a different way.

How Deep Is This Change?

Essayist Wendell Berry, called the "prophet of rural America" by the *New York Times*, is a conservationist, farmer, writer, and English professor. He sees this new viewpoint expressed in our language. "Until the industrial revolution, . . . the dominant images were organic," he notes. "They had to do with living things; they were biological, pastoral, agricultural, or familial. God was seen as a 'shepherd,' the faithful as 'the sheep of His pasture.' One's home country was known as one's 'motherland' . . . Jesus spoke of himself as a 'bridegroom.'

People who took good care of the earth were said to practice 'husbandry.'" In other words, we defined our world in organic, agricultural, and relational terms.

"Now," he writes, "we do not flinch to hear men and women referred to as 'units' as if they were as uniform and interchangeable as machine parts. It is common, and considered acceptable, to refer to the mind as a computer: one's thoughts are 'inputs'; other people's responses are 'feedback.'"[7]

An AIMS staff member, attending a conference with her husband, a public school teacher, heard the guest speaker compare education to an assembly line and students to vehicles. This man is an expert in a field that preaches individuality, requiring teachers to alter lesson plans to accommodate assorted learning styles and disabilities. Yet his language reflected the conviction that children are mere mechanistic systems.

A Technocratic View of God

Technocratic thinking affects the way we look at many things. At the very least, our general population has accepted the notion that information is power. In our data-laden culture, we expect education to transform people. This popular notion presents a theological conundrum, as it seemingly eliminates the need for spiritual transformation through the process of rebirth as described in Scripture.

One of my friends recently met a young man who was called up for military service in Somalia almost a decade ago. When the uncertainty of his situation brought him face to face with his eternal destiny, he started collecting information about various religions, hoping to find one that made sense. Eventually he grew weary, packed up the information, and put it away without ever making a personal decision. My friend told him, "The Bible doesn't say much about information. But it talks a lot about truth. There's a big difference. Information won't set you free, but truth will."

That young man represents a vast number of people in Western culture who seek truth in information. Wendell Berry says our technocratic mindset has an even more insidious effect, because it alters our view of God. He quotes R. Buckminster Fuller, a twentieth century philosopher, inventor, architect, engineer, mathematician, poet, and cosmologist. One of the world's first futurists, Fuller coined the term Spaceship Earth, and he made "synergy" a common part of our vocabulary.

Berry says Fuller "asserted that 'the universe physically is itself the most incredible technology'—the necessary implication being that God is not father, shepherd, or bridegroom, but a mechanic, operating by principles which, according to Fuller, 'can be expressed mathematically.'"[8] That language may speak to our age, but it does not reflect the relational nature of a God who seeks—and finds—the lost.

Organic Imagery in Scripture

We have established that our move from an organic framework to a technological one has shaped many aspects of culture, including our spiritual understanding. I believe most Western Christians have succumbed to this mechanistic paradigm. (A paradigm is a way of thinking. It is like a filter in your brain. As you pass information through it, the filter affects the way you interpret and apply that information. Some experts compare a paradigm to a pair of tinted glasses—just as they color your view of the world, your paradigm colors your view of reality.)

Scripture is based on an agricultural paradigm. The *Dictionary of Biblical Imagery* notes, "From the beginning of the Bible nearly to its end, we move in a predominantly rural and agrarian world of field and vineyard, cattle and herds, sowing and reaping. Although cities exist in the world of the Bible, the majority of the people were directly dependent on the land for their livelihood."[9]

Scripture was lived out among farmers. The land and its bounty dominated life's decisions. Israel's political leaders and prophets sometimes had to leave their fields and/or herds when they accepted their new calling (as in the cases of Saul, David, Elisha, and Amos). Armies would destroy a city and then cover it with salt to render the land infertile, delivering a military deathblow (see Judges 9:45; Psalm 107:34; Jeremiah 48:9). Military officers expressed enticements for surrender in agrarian terms. In Hezekiah's reign, for instance, the Assyrian commander issued this invitation to Jerusalem's multitudes: "Make peace with me and come out to me. Then every one of you will eat from his own vine and fig tree and drink water from his own cistern, until I come and take you to a land like your own, a land of grain and new wine, a land of bread and vineyards, a land of olive trees and honey" (2 Kings 18:31–32).

Since Scripture uses agricultural metaphors also to describe God's plan to grow his kingdom, this leads us to the question: In losing our agricultural paradigm, have we also lost our ability to grasp the effort and method that will cause God's kingdom to take root, grow, and reproduce, spreading over the entire world?

Agricultural Concepts Applied to the Spiritual Realm

Church development specialist Christian A. Schwarz warns

of potential difficulties in applying organic understanding to the supernatural realm. When applied to basic theology, he admits, "It fosters the illusion that we can perceive and understand God on our own—without Christ, without the cross, without revelation." In the realm of church growth, though, he explains, "Learning from creation is not only legitimate, it is a must!"[10]

Some scholars claim that Jesus taught in agricultural parables because he spoke to an agrarian society. "I don't think that goes far enough," Schwarz explains. "If Jesus were walking among us today, he would hardly replace these parables from nature with parables from the world of computers, such as 'The kingdom of God is like a computer program—your output depends on your input.' Technocratic illustrations like this would miss the secret of life."

Laws governing living and non-living things simply are not the same. As Schwarz points out, "A coffee machine can make coffee (thank God!), but it will never make another coffee maker. In nature, however, the order of things is entirely different: a coffee plant produces coffee beans, which in turn can produce new coffee plants."[11]

Schwarz analyzes one of Jesus' metaphors to underscore the value of applying organic principles to spiritual issues. He looks at Matthew 6:28, where Jesus told his followers, "See how the lilies of the field grow." The Greek word translated "see," or "consider" in the KJV, is *katamathete*. It is derived from a Greek word *manthano*, which means "to learn, observe, study, or research." And it has the prefix *kata*, which is used at the beginning of a verb to intensify its meaning. So, in context, the word literally means "to diligently learn, observe, study, or research."

Furthermore, this verse, expressed as a command, says we're not supposed to study the lilies, just admiring beauty and comparing color. Rather, we're supposed to study how they grow—examining the God-ordained principles that govern their natural process of rising from the soil, growing, blooming, and reproducing. Schwarz summarizes, "We are to study them, examine them, meditate on them, and take direction from them—all these aspects are included in the imperative verb form *katamathete*. And we are told that we need to do these things in order to understand the principles of the kingdom of God."[12]

Scripture abounds with similar passages that draw spiritual wisdom from living things. When God created the world, it seems he left a reflection of himself in every particle. (For examples, see Psalm 19:1–4 and Romans 1:19–20.) Thus, God surrounds us with natural parables. When we examine these God-given physical principles in light of Scripture and grasp their meaning, we catch a glimpse of who he is. We also unlock his supernatural plan to glorify himself through the expansion of his kingdom.

God Is a Gardener

Before human history, God planted a garden (Genesis 2:8). This Genesis picture shows God's intimate, physical involvement in developing this garden. Though he could have put Adam anywhere on earth, he put the first man, made in his image, into this garden planted by his own hands. Then he placed Eve there with Adam, so that, together, they would work and take care of the Garden (Genesis 2:15).

Most of us have assumed that if Eve had not convinced Adam to eat the forbidden fruit, they would have stayed forever in that idyllic place. But Scripture says God gave them a mandate. The mandate began with God's blessing for Adam and Eve. The Hebrew word here is *barak*, which means "to kneel." It implies that God came to their level. He initiated the process, kneeling to convey his blessing. From that blessing, he commissioned

Adam and Eve to continue his creative activity by being fruitful and multiplying. Eventually they would fill the entire earth and subdue it. He told them, "Be fruitful and increase in number; fill the earth and subdue it. Rule over the fish of the sea and the birds of the air and over every living creature that moves on the ground" (Genesis 1:28). This was God's first Great Commission, his first command to his people to represent him on earth, and it occurred before Adam and Eve sinned.

Adam and Eve were to work as God's stewards to bring the world and its inhabitants under his dominion for his glory. God used organic terminology to describe how they were to accomplish that.[13]

Be fruitful

The Hebrew word is *parah*, which means "to bear or bring forth fruit or to grow." This word also is used prophetically in Isaiah 17:6 to note that, despite devastation to Damascus, a remnant will survive. God compares that remnant to a few olives left on a fruitful branch. A form of this word is also used in Psalm 107:34, referring to a fruitful land.

Increase in Number

The Hebrew word is *rabah*, meaning "to increase or to bring in abundance." It can also mean "to enlarge, to be full of, or to grow up or heap up." This word is used in Nehemiah 9:37, referring to land yielding an abundant harvest, which was lost to foreign kings because of sin.

The remaining verbs in Genesis 1:28 are not specifically agricultural words, but given the organic context of the first three terms, these last three can have agricultural applications.

Fill the Earth

The Hebrew word for "fill" is *male* (masculine) or *mala* (feminine). It means "to fill or be full of," even to the point of overflowing. It is used, for instance, to describe the action of filling grain sacks and water barrels (Genesis 42:25 and 44:1; 1 Kings 18:33). In an agricultural sense, this overflowing comes naturally from ongoing fruitfulness, each seed producing many more. Some wise person has said, "Any fool can count the seeds in an apple, but only God can count the apples in a seed." Since Adam and Eve were commanded to fill the earth, this implies that the production of more seeds ultimately requires the use of more land.

Subdue It

The Hebrew word for subdue is *kabash*, which means "to tread down, conquer, subjugate, bring into bondage." This is more of a military term than an agricultural term. Yet, in this context of agricultural words, it implies that the natural result of filling and overflowing is the continual subduing of things that limit fruitfulness. Winkie Pratney, a youth evangelist with a background in science and in popular music culture, sees an agricultural link when he writes, "The prolific urge originally implanted in nature to fill and multiply has no built-in moral constraint, no inherent control, no limit. You understand this every time you cultivate a crop. Not only is it not wrong to 'subdue,' but when the ultimate end is to be a harvest or garden—something more beautiful and wonderful than a jungle—it is absolutely necessary."[14]

Rule

The Hebrew word *radah* means "to tread down or subjugate, to crumble off, to prevail against, reign or rule." Again, Pratney notes that this word has a related Hebrew root, *radad,* which carries a connotation in accounting terms of "overlaying or spending." In this context Pratney notes, "To take dominion . . . means not only to win over but to reapportion, to take where there is too much and move it somewhere else."[15] So, even this last word can have an agricultural application in the sense of cultivating and transplanting a crop to a barren place.

The link between the garden and the kingdom is a crucial one that, in large part, has been lost to our twenty-first-century Western mindset. By tending the garden, Adam and Eve would learn how to rule as God's administrators. God gave them tasks and described the tasks in agricultural terms. They were supposed to see the physical parables and discover how to use them for God's glory.

Farmers Growing Grass?

A friend who serves as a missionary to the Ukraine recently traveled through my hometown. We were discussing cultural differences between the two regions, and she commented that her Ukrainian friends were astonished to discover that Americans own so much property that is "unfruitful." I asked what she meant. "Well," she explained, "in Ukraine, anyone with a little bit of ground will grow a garden. In America, most people just have lawns." She could have also mentioned the vast, professionally landscaped areas dedicated to entertainment and relaxation.

Bill Shelton is one farmer who has responded to that trend. Bill, who lives in the Tidewater region of Virginia, took 185 acres where he used to grow soybeans, and instead, he planted grass. In doing so, he joined the state's largest agricultural sector—turfgrass, grown to beautify lawns, roadsides, parks, golf courses, and cemeteries. In fact, turfgrass is one of Virginia's major cash crops, accounting for more than 394,000 jobs in 1998, with an annual payroll of almost $700 million.

Bill Shelton explained, "The grain market has gotten so bad right now that farmers have got to do something." So, in response to a market created by a culture that demands beautiful surroundings without intense personal effort, they grow grass and ornamental plants. After all, Shelton explains, "When people buy a $300,000 home, they don't want to be bothered with mud."[16]

Shelton represents many farmers who are finding it difficult to make a living by growing traditional food crops. They must respond to political and economic shifts, as well as agricultural realities. A friend who is familiar with farming summarized it like this: "A significant portion of agriculture has always been dedicated to something other than food, such as raw materials for fabrics, dyes, medicinal herbs, and fragrances. What has changed is the amount of land that is being used for purely recreational or decorative purposes."

In other words, most of us want beautiful yards, golf courses, theme parks, and the like, as long as someone else puts up with the mud and does the really hard work in the field and in the greenhouse. As my friend explained, "Our farmers are being pressured to find new products, including nursery stock and ornamentals, where they hope to make a profit. Many of these new products cater to the instant gratification elements in our society, but most farmers don't have many other options."

The Spiritual Mirror

Scripture clearly teaches Christians not to *conform* to society's standards. We have a God-given mandate not to mirror our culture, but to *transform* it. Since this book is based on agricultural parables, the notion of farmers growing grass leads to some interesting questions related to local churches and individual Christians.

Have we adopted a spiritual attitude that mirrors our culture's self-indulgent demand of beauty or fruitfulness without personal effort or sacrifice?

Are we more focused on being blessed than on blessing others?

Are we really interested in doing the hard spiritual labor that will yield a spiritual harvest?

Do we even understand what that process will require?

The title of this book is based on John Milton's classic poem *Paradise Lost*, which describes Adam and Eve's loss of Eden. Similarly, we live in a culture that has moved far from the garden—figuratively and literally. That change has affected us in many ways, including a loss of understanding related to spiritual harvest. We must grasp the same lessons that would have helped Adam and Eve fulfill their calling. It is a long trip back, and it is full of twists and turns and barricades. Understanding spiritual harvest may require us to lay aside technocratic assumptions and think like farmers.

I'm convinced that Christians in general, and Christian leaders in particular, must return to an agricultural paradigm as it applies to the way we do God's work in this world. The return trip may not be easy, but it will be worth the effort. We must recover a lost paradigm—the agricultural, organic, natural growth paradigm as it relates to spiritual issues—if we are truly going to grow God's kingdom in the way he intended.

Sow This Book into Your Life

1. Describe some ways that technocratic or mechanistic thinking has been applied to overall church growth strategies.

_____

_____

2. How has that mechanistic paradigm affected your own spiritual journey and your understanding of God's plan for evangelism and missions? How has it affected your church?

_____

_____

3. Re-read the explanation of the Hebrew words in Genesis 1:28. Describe how that progression can be expressed in terms of a church development strategy.

_____

_____

4. In answering a questionnaire distributed to church leaders, a pastor for student ministries and missions in Port St. Lucie, Florida, noted that harvest "includes ever expanding your fields into areas untouched, ungroomed, and untilled before. Harvest includes the potential harvest that awaits in and from areas that man may see as dry, barren and infertile." He added, "As a church, we are not satisfied to work and rework the same field, but [we want] to venture out to new harvest fields [where] God is leading us." Explain how his answer fits the picture of Genesis 1:28.

_____

_____

5. The end of this chapter asks some important questions. According to your current knowledge, answer them for yourself and for your church:

- Have we adopted a spiritual attitude that mirrors our culture's self-indulgent demand of beauty and fruitfulness without personal effort or sacrifice?

_____

- Are we more focused on being blessed than on blessing others?

_____

- Are we really interested in doing the hard spiritual labor that will yield a spiritual harvest?

_____

- Do we even understand what that process will require?

_____

In preparation for chapter 2, read:

Deuteronomy 11

chapter 2 < lord of the land

Our experiences give us a unique perspective that influences our viewpoint. That's why, if five people witness an accident, you may get five very different accounts of the event. It's even true of our view of Scripture. The Bible was written when most people were farmers. But most contemporary Westerners aren't farmers. We grow a few vegetables. We lavish attention on our flowers. But most of all, at least in the United States, we are infatuated with our lawns.

Ruth, my co-writer, grew up in the country, and then lived in a city. Now her family has moved to a suburban subdivision. It's a whole new experience. "In the country and in the city, we made a little effort to keep our lawns healthy," she said. "We might spread lime once a year and battle certain pests, but mostly we just mowed off whatever came up. In my new neighborhood, lawns are the hot topic of conversation. We compare successes and failures. We decide who has the best grass, and we discuss whether they accomplished that lush, green lawn by themselves or hired someone to do it for them."

She speaks to the thousands of acres of U.S. soil, primarily in sprawling suburbia, that is devoted to lawns. Lawn planting and maintenance, which require more equipment, labor, fuel and agricultural chemicals than all other farming in the United States, is the largest single agricultural sector in the U.S. and perhaps on the whole planet. Some agricultural experts say U.S. lawns require "more resources than any other agricultural industry in the world."[1]

Besides that, we saturate lawns with massive amounts of water, so that in areas such as the American Southwest, lawns pose a serious threat to adequate water supply. We couple that with using more pesticides, herbicides, and other "cides" on our lawns than in any other form of agriculture. And when we combine those chemicals with all that water, we contribute greatly to pollution through the run-off.[2] As one author stated, "There is cause for alarm. A lot of technology is now hooking our dependency even deeper to 'the _____cides': pesticides, fungicides, weedicides, insecticides. Five billion pounds of poisons are . . . manufactured by chemical companies each year, lethal substances that must go somewhere and go most often into our air, soil, or water."[3]

After traveling extensively in the developing world, I am not eager to return to days with no vehicles or electricity, no indoor plumbing or clean drinking water, no telephones, fax machines or e-mail, and no adequate medical care. But I readily admit that progress has its limitations. It has negative impacts as well as positive, especially as it destroys our sense of community and poisons our environment. I am not an ecological expert. But, based on my research, I want to explore how our spiritual belief system reflects our physical view of the environment.

The Spiritual Environment

When I launched into ministry, I helped pioneer Teen Challenge outreaches in Europe, Asia, and the Middle East. I was invited to visit Sweden to preach in Scandinavia's largest free church. Louis Petrus pastored this congregation, which birthed a renewal that spread throughout Sweden and Finland, influencing Norway as well and initiating a widespread grass-roots missionary outreach. I asked Brother Petrus why his church was such a powerhouse for God's kingdom. He was in his late 70s and had retired. His eyes twinkled as he answered with one word—environment. He didn't mean Scandinavia's physical environment. He meant the spiritual environment of his church and of the culture that surrounded it. Our success in growing God's kingdom rests largely on our understanding of spiritual environment. Western culture has moved away from the farmer's mindset. As noted in the previous chapter, we see this trend in the United States where general society has replaced the ideal of food production with the contentment of beautifying our postage-stamp lawns. The church will die if we duplicate this in the spiritual sense. We need to look at the Bible and the world through a farmer's eyes.

Where Do We Start?

Let's begin with the basics as they relate to Israel. After all, this is where Scripture was written.

Israel is a small place—about 150 miles from north to south, with the Dead Sea (close to the eastern border) being only fifty miles from the Mediterranean Sea on the west. In biblical days Israel was regarded primarily as a corridor for travel to somewhere else. If land value is based on "location, location, location," Israel was prime property. It sat at the trading crossroads between Mesopotamia and Egypt—a perfect spot for spreading ideas and impacting cultures.

Respected biblical scholar Alfred Edersheim notes that biblical Palestine "combined every variety of climate," from snow in the mountains to the "genial warmth of the Lake of Galilee and the tropical heat of the Jordan Valley."[4] Israel's topographical variations, coupled with its location near the Mediterranean Sea, contribute to irregular weather patterns. Temperatures fluctuate between seasons, with Jerusalem averaging about fifty degrees in January (the coldest month) and seventy-seven degrees in August (the hottest month). Some parts of Israel see occasional frost in winter, and it is not uncommon for Jerusalem to have snow. But more than temperature, water availability sets the limit for agricultural seasons.

Israel's higher altitudes generally get more rain. The southern desert sees negligible precipitation, and the lowlands attract less rainfall than the hill country and mountains. Thus, in a normal year, the mountains north of Galilee receive considerably more moisture than Judea's hills. In an average year, the highlands receive about the same amount of rain as Great Britain, but instead of spreading it out over the whole year, the highlands get it all in about six months—and it won't be distributed evenly. Rainfall increases, peaks, and decreases, so that 70 percent of all rain falls from December through February.

By contrast, summer is a season of consistency—as one author described it, "clear skies, regular sea breezes, and minimal temperature fluctuations."[5] Summer is dry, so winter was the primary growing season for the biblical farmer. In Palestine, plowing began when the first rains softened the soil in October or November. Winter rains were heavy and cold, so farmers faced the temptation of waiting for warmer weather. That's why Proverbs 20:4 warns, "A sluggard does not plow in season, so at harvest time he looks but finds nothing."

They sowed wheat then, since it required the longest growing season. Barley followed, along with millet, lentils, peas, melons, and cucumbers. The Israelites also planted a variety of vegetables; they grew and harvested grapes, almonds, figs, olives, dates, and pomegranates. From December through February, farmers cultivated the crops to keep them weed-free. Then, as temperatures rose, winter downpours gave way to spring showers in March and April. These last rains caused the grain to mature and swell. If everything went according to schedule, by the end of April, the barley crop, first to be harvested each year, was ready.

The Environment Bred Uncertainty

Israel's topography and climate, however, bred uncertainty of agricultural success. When Moses was preparing the Israelites to enter the Promised Land, he told them, "The LORD your God is bringing you into a good land . . . a land with wheat and barley, vines and fig trees, pomegranates, olive oil and honey; a land where bread will not be scarce and you will lack for nothing." (Deuteronomy 8:7–9). One author noted it "provided a good environment . . . to learn lessons about God, the Creator and Provider. The land depended on him sending the all-important rains and keeping away locusts and famine. And the landscape quickly showed up any folly or greed on the part of the people who occupied it. Soil erosion, the loss of trees and shrubs, wells drying up, or fields losing their fertility, all showed that things were going wrong among the people in a land that was supposed to 'flow with milk and honey.'"[6]

The Israelites found themselves in a place that lacked the agricultural certainty of Mesopotamia and Egypt. In Mesopotamia, a healthy agricultural system had been sustained for centuries through irrigation systems and technologically advanced farm implements of stone and flint. In Egypt, the Nile's annual flooding watered the land well and enriched the soil with silt from the river bottom. Egyptians also developed irrigation systems for dry periods.[7]

Canaan wasn't like that. Here, harvests depended on winter rains, which varied from year to year and even from place to place. Because of topographical variances, annual rainfall can be significantly greater on one side of a mountain than on the other side of the same mountain. Scholars have compared the northern highlands to "a climatic battlefield where opposing forces of sea and desert meet head on." [8]

As he prepared them for this new venture, Moses warned the people, "The land you are entering . . . is not like the land of Egypt, from which you have come, where you planted your seed and irrigated it by foot as in a vegetable garden. But the land you are crossing the Jordan to take possession of is a land of mountains and valleys that drinks rain from heaven" (Deuteronomy 11:10–11).

Trusting and Obeying God

Moses said the Hebrews' security rested in God alone. They were to obey him, love him, and serve him. The result would be his provision. "[T]hen I will send rain on your land in its season, both autumn and spring rains, so that you may gather in your grain, new wine, and oil. I will provide grass in the fields for your cattle, and you will eat and be satisfied" (Deuteronomy 11:14–15). The Israelites were not to succumb to the Canaanites' attempts to control and manipulate the environment by appeasing Baal—the storm god. "Be careful," Moses warned, "or you will be enticed to turn away and worship other gods and bow down to them. Then the LORD's anger will burn against you, and he will shut the heavens so that it will not rain and the ground will yield no produce, and you will soon perish" (Deuteronomy 11:16–17).

Rainfall was only one concern. Locusts, sometimes numbering in the millions, swarmed through the land, eating every green plant (see Judges 6:5; Joel 2). Though the rains were a blessing, they also eroded soil, so land had to be terraced in retaining walls. This was not an easy place to farm, but God promised that obedience would bring his protection and provision.

The Promised Land Was a Gift

This is the environment where God placed his people—the group he chose to reflect his way in a fallen world. This was the environment where God placed the very people who would give birth to the Messiah. This was the environment where God initiated his plan, prophesied all the way back at the Garden, when he foretold the birth of Eve's eventual offspring who would crush Satan's head (see Genesis 3:14–15). That child was Jesus. God placed his Son in this land, inhabited by a people he selected, not because they deserved it, but just because he wanted it done that way.

Wendell Berry calls it a gift. He sees a "vein of light" in the Deuteronomy account of God's preparing the Israelites to inhabit Palestine. "This light," he explains, "originates in the idea of the land as a gift. . . . It is a gift because the people who are to possess it did not create it." He cites Leviticus 25:23 in which God declares that he owns the land, and the Israelites are simply his tenants. Berry notes, "In this warning we have the root of the idea of propriety, of proper human purposes and ends. We must not use the world as though we had created it ourselves."[9]

Berry explains, "What is given is not ownership, but . . . the right of habitation and use." Even that can be taken away, for the Promised Land was not given as a reward for good behavior. Berry concludes, "The people chosen for this gift do not deserve it, for they are 'a stiff-necked people' who have been wicked and faithless. To such a people such a gift can be given only as a moral predicament: having failed to deserve it beforehand, they must prove worthy of it afterwards; they must use it well, or they will not continue long in it."[10]

How will they prove themselves worthy? By obeying the rules God established to govern their behavior. These rules, covered in large part in the Bible's first five books, give extensive answers to almost every moral dilemma. Berry says they can basically be summarized in three statements:

The Israelites Must Remember That The Land Is a Gift

Moses summarized it like this: "When you have eaten and are satisfied, praise the LORD your God for the good land he has given you. Be careful that you do not forget the LORD your God." (Deuteronomy 8:10–11).

They Must Be Neighborly

They must treat people with respect, kindness, and honesty. Berry says, "These are social virtues, but . . . they have ecological and agricultural implications." He explains that "the land is described as an 'inheritance.'" Within this context, the commands regarding kindness to others also take in future generations. Berry admits, "We can have no direct behavioral connection to those who are not yet alive. The only neighborly thing we can do for them is to preserve their inheritance: we must take care . . . of the land, which is never a possession, but an inheritance to the living, as it will be to the unborn."[11]

They Must Practice Good Husbandry

Berry notes verses like Deuteronomy 22:6–7, which state that anyone who finds a nest with a mother bird and babies can take the young ones but must leave the mother. Berry concludes, "This . . . is a perfect paradigm of ecological and agricultural discipline. . . . The inflexible rule is that the source must be preserved. You may take the young, but you must save the breeding stock. You may eat the harvest, but you must save seed, and you must preserve the fertility of the fields."[12]

Spiritual Ecology

Wendell Berry is steadfast in his ecological views. Some would question the extent to which he avoids technology and recommends traditional tools and methods for the sake of protecting the environment. Still, he makes a point that largely has been ignored by our culture in general and by churches in particular. God ordained his people to be the world's caretakers.

Winkie Pratney notes a certain reluctance on the part of many Western Christians to ascribe to a theology that includes responsibility for our physical environment. Citing scientific advancements which reveal more and more about our environment, Pratney describes the church like this: "Equipped as never before with new windows on the nature of reality, the group of people best qualified to conduct the orchestra did not even hear the music. God spoke, they heard his voice in the Garden and were afraid and hid themselves. . . . They covered their spiritual nakedness with the fig leaves of formal tradition and left the study of Eden to people better acquainted with snakes and the Tree of Knowledge than the Tree of Life."[13]

Pratney's comments address what he sees as reluctance on the part of many Christians to address issues related to our physical environment. But is there a similar reluctance to face our responsibilities related to our spiritual environment? God has placed every believer and every local church in a spiritual "land." Our stewardship of resources will help determine the fruitfulness, but the land itself is his gift, as well as the resources we use to subdue it, as described in the previous chapter. Every Christian's spiritual land—the place where he is to plant seeds, tend plants, and eventually reap a harvest—includes his own culture, similar cultures, and cultures that are entirely different from his own. God will lead each Christian and/or church to the field(s) he wants to give them.

But we must always remember that it is his gift. He owns the land, he cares for it, and he provides for and protects it. He gives us the honor of being his stewards—his servants, responsible for keeping his property according to his standards.

That influences the type of spiritual seed we sow and how we manage the harvest. It helps us decide if we are going to grow food for the spiritually hungry, or if we are going to settle for keeping well-manicured spiritual lawns. The understanding of God's ownership and our stewardship forces one simple question: Are we growing his kingdom, or our own?

The Joy of Tending God's Garden

Steve Hayner, when he was president of InterVarsity Christian Fellowship, published an editorial in *World Christian* magazine entitled "The Joy of Tending God's Garden." Hayner notes that God could evangelize the world all by himself. For some reason, he invites us to work with him in the ministry of reconciling the world to himself (2 Corinthians 5:18–20).

Hayner compares God's desire to his own experience of gardening with his son.

> I knew that if we did this together, the job would take longer, the rows wouldn't be as straight as if I did them myself, and he would get dirty, maybe even hurt himself. But I said yes, and the partnership we shared was intense. I still have a picture of him standing beside the planted rows, with sweaty face, bandaged finger

and smudged clothes. And a smile of sheer delight.

God is calling us to that kind of partnership—working together to carry out his mission. He knows the task will not be done as quickly as if he did it himself. He knows we will get hurt and dirty. And still he lets us share in the sowing the seeds of the gospel, out of his willingness to share the joy of fellowship with us. At the same time, he gets glory out of it, too. "But we have this treasure in jars of clay to show that this all-surpassing power is from God and not from us."[14]

Sow This Book into Your Life

1. This chapter discusses the concept of spiritual environment. A senior pastor at a church in Oakdale, California, described his church's overall strategy to us like this:

- Attract the interest of the lost.
- Demonstrate the love of God and the power of the gospel.
- Share the truth of the gospel in the power of the Holy Spirit.
- Train soul winners and trainers of soul winners.

What does that list tell you about the spiritual environment at his church?

_____

_____

_____

2. Describe the spiritual environment at your church.

_____

_____

_____

3. As recorded in Deuteronomy, God informed the Hebrew people that he owned the land of Palestine, but he was giving them the right of tenancy. In a spiritual sense, God also owns the lands that he assigns to you, but he gives you the right of habitation or tenancy. Is that understanding freeing or limiting? How does it impact your commitment to steward the land into fruitfulness on God's behalf?

_____

_____

_____

4. Re-read Wendell Berry's list of implications that rose from the Israelites' understanding that God owns the land. Describe how those implications also have merit in the ministry God has assigned to you:

- In remembering that the "land" is a gift:

_____

_____

- In being neighborly, treating people with respect, kindness, and honesty:

_____

_____

- In practicing good husbandry and principles of good stewardship:

_____

_____

5. If God has the ability to evangelize the world all on his own, why does he want us to be involved in the process? What is the impact of your obedience to his plan?

_____

_____

6. This chapter makes this observation: "The understanding of God's ownership and our stewardship forces one simple question: Are we growing his kingdom, or our own?" Answer that question for yourself and for your church.

_____

_____

In preparation for chapter 3, read:

Leviticus 25

P   A   R   A

chapter 3 < lord of time

L ights. Camera. Action.

Acting legend Jimmy Stewart enters through a doorway in the classic movie *Shenandoah*, filmed in 1965. Six lanky strides take him to the far end of a family table, set for dinner. Seven young adults (five men and two women) stand reverently behind chairs on both sides. At the table's end, Stewart right-faces and moves to his chair. His gray hair glints in the warm interior light, and his blue eyes squint with the steady determination—some would say stubbornness—that has enabled him to raise a healthy, strong family as a widowed father.

In this scene, the movie invites the viewer to eavesdrop on the family's dinner. You watch Stewart from the opposite end of the long table. He is a profoundly moral, church-going man, genuinely committed to hard work. His youngest son, about sixteen years old, arrives late from a fishing adventure, interrupting the father's mealtime prayer. Stewart continues. "Lord," he says, "we cleared this land. We plowed it, sowed it, and harvested it. We cooked the harvest. It wouldn't be here, and we wouldn't be eating it, if we hadn't done it all ourselves. We worked dog-bone hard for every crumb and morsel, but we thank you just the same, Lord, for this food we're about to eat. Amen."

This "blessing" is really a litany of personal effort—perhaps even a backhanded list of grievances against a God who didn't ease the labor. Then again, maybe Stewart's character is just a more honest pray-er than most of us. We can fall into the same trap. We can lose sight of God's true place in our lives *and* in our work, even when that work is on *his* land and in *his* field.

The Promised Land Revisited

Israel's location, where three continents intersect, is a meeting ground for plants and wildlife from places as diverse as Siberia, Western Europe, inner Asia, and North and East Africa. It is home to about three thousand species of plants. Compare that to eighteen hundred species in Britain (two-and-a-half times larger than Israel), or fifteen hundred species in Egypt (ten times larger, and home to one of the Middle East's most fertile areas, the Nile delta.)[1] We get a hint of Israel's agricultural wealth from the twelve spies sent out by Moses. "When they reached the Valley of Eshcol," Scripture tells us, "they cut off a branch bearing a single cluster of grapes." That cluster required two men to carry it. The spies reported, "We went into the land to which you sent us, and it does flow with milk and honey!" Pointing to the grapes, as well as to pomegranates and figs they brought with them, they said, "Here is its fruit" (Numbers 13:23, 27).

In that environment, a good harvest could lead to the same assertion prayed aloud in *Shenandoah*. We all can succumb to the assumption that success and bounty grow naturally from our own hard work. Moses recognized that potential, so in preparing the Israelites to enter the Promised Land, he told them:

> When you have eaten and are satisfied, praise the LORD your God for the good land he has given you. Be careful that you do not forget the LORD your God, failing to observe his commands, his laws and his

decrees . . . Otherwise, when you eat and are satisfied,
. . . when your herds and flocks grow large and your
silver and gold increase and all you have is multiplied,
then your heart will become proud and you will forget
the LORD your God. . . . You may say to yourself, "My
power and the strength of my hands have produced
this wealth for me." But remember the LORD your
God, for it is he who gives you the ability to produce
wealth, and so confirms his covenant, which he swore
to your forefathers, as it is today. (Deuteronomy
8:10–14, 17–18)

Do You Have a Shenandoah Attitude?

If this movie had existed in Moses' time, he could have
summarized that passage by saying, "Don't give way to a
Shenandoah attitude. Recognize God's place in your life and in
your work. Trust him to supply the resources, and then steward
them into fruitfulness for his glory."

In Israel's life, the expression of this reliance on the Lord
of the universe—the God who created and chose them—was
perhaps best expressed in honoring his stipulations regarding
what I call "the biblical sevens." These mandates required them
to rest from their work and trust his provision.

The Seventh Day of the Week

This day is called the Sabbath, from the primitive Hebrew
root *shabbath*, which means "to repose, to desist from
exertion."[2] The Israelites were commanded to "remember
the Sabbath day by keeping it holy." According to Exodus
20:8–11, the Sabbath was set aside not just as a time to cease
working, but also as a time to fellowship with God.

The Seventh Year

God planned a regular period of rest for both his people and for the land. "For six years sow your fields," he said. "And for six years prune your vineyards and gather their crops. But in the seventh year the land is to have a sabbath of rest, a sabbath to the LORD. Do not sow your fields or prune your vineyards. Do not reap what grows of itself or harvest the grapes of your untended vines. The land is to have year of rest" (Leviticus 25:3–5).

The Year of Jubilee

This event occurred every fifty years. God told his people, "Consecrate the fiftieth year and proclaim liberty throughout the land to all its inhabitants. It shall be a jubilee for you" (Leviticus 25:10). Once again, the land was to rest. Planting or harvesting was outlawed. Technically, the Year of Jubilee would be the second year in a row for this type of injunction, since it followed the forty-ninth year, which would have been one of the sevens. Yet God promised to provide, despite the lack of farming. In addition, God required the Israelites to return property to its rightful owners, to forgive debts, and to free slaves.

The Biblical Understanding of Rest

In our technocratic busy-ness, most Westerners have lost the ideal of rest. Seminary professor and Old Testament scholar John Oswalt sees the loss of leisure in all contemporary life. "My grandfather farmed with a team of mules," he notes. "Every fall it took him ten weeks—from the middle of September until the end of November—to plow and plant 150 acres of winter wheat, and that was working dawn to dusk.

But I suspect he was more leisured than I." He adds, "With all of the labor-saving devices at our beck and call, it seems that we ought to have nothing to do. But in fact many of us are run ragged." He concludes, "There seem to be more things clamoring for our time than we can possibly handle. . . . This is the crisis of our times. . . . The question is not *whether* we shall fill the time. We will do that, like it or not. No, the question is *how* we shall fill it."[3]

Leonard Sweet describes this same trend as he outlines the freedom Americans gained by doing away with that which inhibited business activities on Sundays. "And what 'freedoms' we enjoy," he writes. "'Freedom' to work seven-day weeks. 'Freedom' to take 'working vacations,' 'working breakfasts,' 'working lunches,' 'working dinners.' 'Freedom' to be dog collared to electronic ball-and-chains so that no one can get away from work . . ."

He adds, "Our freedom from the 'Sabbath' exacted a high toll. When we lost Sabbaths, we lost spiritual well-being. It is not so much that we 'keep the Sabbath' as the Sabbath keeps us—keeps us whole, keeps us sane, keeps us spiritually alive. Genuine Sabbath-keeping is not a series of 'you shall nots' but a string of celebrations. Its goal is not to shut you off from the realities of life, but to open you up to living."[4]

The Benefit of the Fallow Year

Most of us know that rest is crucial for human beings. The Bible says even the land must rest. The fallow year, when land that is usually cultivated is allowed to remain idle, improves the soil in ways that even chemical fertilizers and pesticides cannot quite achieve, restoring trace elements that cannot be fully renewed through ordinary cultivation. It breaks the life cycle of certain plant diseases, reduces infestation of harmful insects, and renews the effects of earthworms, benign insects, and other life forms that actually improve soil fertility.

God worked this requirement of rest into all of creation, and he was quite determined to see his people honor this requirement. Israel's historians recorded Jerusalem's fall and the Babylonian captivity in Second Chronicles, explaining that during this exile "the land enjoyed its sabbath rests; all the time of its desolation it rested until the seventy years were completed" (2 Chronicles 36:21). One commentator says God was "presumably making up for a half-millennium of neglected sabbatic years."[5]

Implications for Spiritual Harvest

After examining the scriptural mandates and the physical evidence, I cannot escape the fact that God's injunctions related to rest, for both the farmer and the land, must have bearing for growing God's kingdom. I've wrestled with applications. I'll leave it to individual missionaries, evangelists, pastors, mission boards, and congregations to develop standards allowing seasons of rest for individuals. In the corporate sense, though, as it relates to the global body of Christ allowing the "land" to rest, I don't believe God wants all of his followers to take simultaneous vacations from sharing the gospel and discipling believers.

David C. Hopkins, who has studied farming in Israel during the Iron Age, gives agricultural evidence that supports my position. He notes that while Hebrew farmers did not plant or harvest crops in the fallow year—the seventh year or the Year of Jubilee—the land was not entirely idle. At the very least, he explains, farmers often turned fallow fields into pasturelands. This gave them the benefit of manure without the intense labor involved in spreading it. It also helped to control the weeds.[6]

That practice implies that God continues to grow his kingdom, even in a time when he requires rest. Thus, I believe the Sabbath laws were not arbitrary commandments designed to limit the freedom of God's people. Rather, they gave specific application to the principle of resting in God through obedience to his will. In the book of Joshua, for example, God told the Israelites to march around Jericho for seven days (see Joshua 6). One of those days must have been a Sabbath. Similarly, the New Testament notes that many of Jesus' miracles, which grew his kingdom immeasurably, were accomplished on Sabbaths. That is one reason he was always in trouble with religious leaders.

Furthermore, according to Hebrews 4, the Sabbath foreshadows the rest offered through a trusting relationship with God through Christ. The passage crescendos through a comparison to the Hebrew wanderers who received God's promise, yet failed to enter the Promised Land, thus missing their rest because they lacked faith in God's ability to release the land from its current inhabitants. The author builds to verses 9–11: "There remains, then, a Sabbath-rest for the people of God; for anyone who enters God's rest also rests from his own work, just as God did from his. Let us, therefore, make every effort to enter that rest, so that no one will fall by following [the Israelites'] example of disobedience."

This passage uses a possessive form to indicate that rest belongs to God. It further describes rest as a cessation of work based on God's example at creation. However, as explained in *The New Testament Study Bible*, "God's rest was not a cessation of all his activity. He ceased his creation, but he continued to sustain it and take an active part and interest in it."[7]

Thus, the implication of the Sabbath rest does not necessarily require us to stop all activity, but it does require that we quit trying to accomplish God's work according to our own agenda and timetable, and in our own strength. Rest is a matter of faith.

So, we're back to the question that provides the starting point for this entire book. What does this all mean to the total process of evangelism and missions?

Every individual Christian and every local church plays a crucial role in God's plan to grow his global kingdom, but no one individual Christian or local church has the full responsibility. Too many people are either jaded or worn out because they feel they must respond to every plea that arises from God's gargantuan estate.

Strategy Breeds Rest

God alone has the ability to oversee the entire, global harvest. In his grace, he assigns each of us to a field or task. When we stand humbly before him and seek his will, he gives us a specific call. This falls under the "good works, which God prepared in advance for us to do" (Ephesians 2:10).

The most basic secret of rest, then, is to get a handle on the specific "works" that God has assigned to us. This is the strategy that breeds rest. How does strategy breed rest?

First, God always provides us with the strength and resources to accomplish his will, so that we will be able to operate in his power rather than our own. Second, when we have God's plan, we have the right to say "no" to activities that fall outside that strategy. It does not mean those activities are not legitimate needs. Rather, it means God has planned for someone else to meet them, and we can trust him to provide that person.

So, I believe in God-given strategy. I'll go even further.

- I believe in vision and mission statements.
- I believe in measurable goals and objectives.
- I believe in schedules and timelines.

But, while those things make great servants, they are equally lousy masters. Honoring the Sabbath means that God remains my master, and he has the right to interrupt my schedule. He even has the right to tell me to "be still."

In chapter two, we explored the idea that God owns the land. But the message of the Sabbath is that God also owns time. Though he lives outside of it, he created it, and he ordained that we would live in a world governed by it. He gives it as a gift—one of many resources that we are to steward into fruitfulness.

Our Western world is time-conscious. In his book *Redeeming the Time: A Christian Approach to Work and Leisure,* Leland Ryken notes, "It is impossible to overemphasize the difference that the advent of the clock brought into Western life. Prior to the mechanical measurement of time, life was lived according to the natural rhythm of the day. Sunrise and sunset determined one's daily schedule. With time measured in such large blocks, and with work ceasing at nightfall, life was generally felt to be less pressured than it is today."

He adds, "Today we measure time in increasingly smaller units, and we typically slice the entire twenty-four-hour period into time units. A decade ago a national magazine ran a cover article on time in which the cover carried a sketch of a person's head with a clock inside. This is, in fact, how most adults live their lives, constantly conscious of the passing of time and of where they are on a time schedule. Above all, time has become a quantity, and this situation has produced a schedule-dominated life."[8]

The Sabbath attitude demands that we leave a lifestyle dominated by schedules so we can live according to God's understanding of time.

Chronos vs. Kairos

The New Testament uses two very different words to refer to time. The first, *chronos*, refers to the measured time that drives our day-timers. It is the root that gives us the word "chronology." In his book *Living Out the Book of Acts*, Bruce Larson explains, "If we think we have only that dimension, we end up being what doctors call Type A personalities, driven workaholics prone to cardiovascular problems and heart attacks. Most of us are all too aware that we've got only so much measurable time, so we get up earlier and work harder to accomplish our goals."[9]

Scripture also describes another kind of time. In Greek, it's called *kairos*. In English, we translate it "in the fullness of time," or "the moment of opportunity." Kairos is that perfect spiritual opportunity when God organizes everything and then throws open the door, inviting us to walk through with him.

Jesus' life and ministry were marked by kairos time rather than chronos time, and he commanded his disciples to imitate his example. Bruce Larson explains, "After Jesus' ascension, they went back to the Upper Room where they had celebrated the Last Supper with him and there they waited. They could accomplish nothing until the power came. . . .When the kairos comes, you're on God's agenda; the door opens and you go through it and give it all you've got."[10]

Kairos has its most obvious application in spiritual matters. But let me give you a baseball illustration to clear up any lingering misunderstanding.

Earl Weaver managed the Baltimore Orioles from 1968 till 1982, and then again from 1985 till 1986. He required his players to refrain from stealing bases unless he gave the appropriate sign. Reggie Jackson thought he was better able to determine whether he could safely make it to second base, so in one game he defied the rule. Based on his understanding, he stole second—and he succeeded.

But Weaver later took him aside and explained why he had not given the steal sign. The next batter was Lee May, second only to Jackson in power hitting for the Orioles. When Jackson stole second base, that left first base empty, so the opposing team intentionally walked May, denying any opportunity for him to hurt them with an extra-base hit. The batter following May had not been particularly strong against the opposing pitcher. With two men on base, Weaver felt compelled to use a pinch hitter, which left him without the bench strength needed later in the game.

Jackson saw the situation only as it affected him. But Weaver had the big picture. You could say that if Jackson had followed Weaver's rule, accepting that his manager had a better viewpoint for making decisions, he could have operated on kairos time. Instead he settled for chronos time, working from his own schedule. Though he was safe at second, he effectively upset the entire game plan.[11]

A Christian who can rely on kairos time has learned to submit to God, not just as Lord of the land, but also as Lord of the time. That is the essence of the Sabbath.

"Rest As If All Your Work Is Done"

The final application comes from Jewish scholar Abraham Heschel. He notes that, in the human world, work is never really done. Because we cannot tie up every loose end in just six days, our work is always incomplete. But, when God issued the Ten Commandments including one requiring a day of rest each week, he was admonishing mankind to "rest . . . as if all your work were done."[12]

How does that apply to our work of evangelism and missions? We live and labor in the world of the "in-between." Ken Blue, a seasoned pastor, church planter, and missionary, describes this paradox with a historical example from World War II. "On 'D-Day,'" he recalls, "the allied troops landed successfully at Normandy beach in order to establish a secure beach-head on the European mainland. It was understood by military experts . . . that this operation secured ultimate victory for the allies. There would be, however, many more bloody battles fought before the day on which ultimate victory would be realized."[13] After military forces fully subdued the enemy, the Allies were able to celebrate a victory that, in actuality, was won on European beaches on D-Day but was celebrated later on VE-Day (Victory in Europe Day).

In a spiritual sense, we live and labor in that period between D-Day and V-Day. The eternal battle for God's kingdom was won through Jesus' sacrificial death almost two thousand years ago. That was the spiritual D-Day, when Jesus said, "It is finished."

Now we are engaged in the process of enforcing his victory as we spread the good news of freedom to every people group in the world. And God's Word assures us that V-Day is already "in the works." We'll deal with this in more detail later, but for now, here are a few of God's promises related to this victory:

- Habakkuk 2:14 tells us "the earth will be filled with the knowledge of the glory of the LORD, as the waters cover the sea."

- Mark 13:10 says the gospel will be preached to every people group before Jesus returns.

- John's Revelation notes that heaven will be populated by people of every tribe, tongue, and nation—people who have accepted a new identity as a "kingdom of priests" (5:9–10, 7:9).

Although we are still actualizing the spiritual D-Day, we can do it with a Sabbath attitude—we can rest in the fact that Jesus has done the hard part. While we grow his kingdom, we can do it with the understanding that, in many ways, the work is already done.

Tony Campolo, building on this same theme, writes, "We live between God's D-Day and His V-Day. We must grasp the good news that we are now dealing with a defeated enemy whose eventual destruction has been assured. Even as we see the hand of the Evil One at work all around us, we have incredible hope."[14] That hope is the essence of Sabbath rest, even in the midst of spiritual labor.

Sow This Book Into Your Life

1. On a scale of 1–10, with 1 being no emphasis at all and 10 being total attention, mark your personal commitment to your calendar or your day-timer. Circle the number that best reflects your answer.

1   2   3   4   5   6   7   8   9   10

2. Describe your personal schedule and your church schedule. Then ask yourself these questions:

- What does my personal schedule reveal about the presence or absence of an overall strategy?

- What about my church schedule?

- If I, or my church, have a spiritual strategy, what is the primary goal that guides the planning?

- Does my personal schedule reflect a reliance on *chronos* or *kairos* time?

- What about my church schedule?

3. Strategy begins with an overall goal. Some people call this a mission or vision statement. An aide to the senior pastor at a church in Hampton, Virginia, says his church exists "to be a community of loving disciples who are bold in faith, strong in character, global in vision, proclaiming the good news of Jesus Christ." That statement reflects the kind of goal that will undergird a successful strategy. It gives an overall picture of the target.

Later we'll address the process of developing a strategy. For now, take time to write out your overall life goal and that of your church. It will be the starting point for your plan of action. After all, you have to know where you are going before you can figure out how to get there. And keep in mind that your mission and vision don't have to be set in stone; they may grow as you study Scripture and read this book.

_____

_____

_____

_____

In preparation for chapter 4, read:

Leviticus 23

P A R A

chapter 4 < the lord of harvest

ntoinette Russell got more than she bargained for when she bought a microwave stand from an auction house for only three dollars. Cleaning out the accumulated trash, Antoinette found eight autograph books full of signatures. These were not everyday, run-of-the-mill, school girlfriend autographs; these were signatures from Muhammad Ali, Richard Pryor, John Lennon, Yoko Ono, Ron Howard, Marion Anderson, Minnie Pearl, Sally Struthers, Sammy Davis Jr., George C. Scott, and Bette Davis. You see, Antoinette's table once belonged to a woman who regularly stood outside the studios of Mike Douglas's variety show, collecting autographs from celebrity guests.

Antoinette's purchase skyrocketed in value, from three dollars to three thousand dollars—all because someone finally looked beyond the obvious and discovered what was inside.[1]

The "Inside Scoop"

Like Antoinette's microwave stand, many things in life seem to gain value, or at least interest, through careful investigation. To some, studying Israel's feasts in Leviticus might seem boring. After all, Leviticus reads like a primer on personal behavior. It outlines injunctions against certain sexual practices and reiterates the Ten Commandments and also describes how to handle various skin diseases and deal with mildew. But if we look beyond the surface, we will discover its value.

I found value in studying Israel's holidays. As outlined in Leviticus 23 and repeated in Deuteronomy 16, the celebrations included three basic seasons which we know as Passover, Pentecost, and the Feast of Booths or Tabernacles.

In researching these three feast seasons, I found enough information to support a book on each one. Their overtones begin in history and end in prophecy. Some feasts point to Jesus' Messianic ministry. Others relate to the birth and growth of the global Church, while others seem to prophesy Jesus' triumphant second coming. For this book, however, I want to look specifically at these festivals as they relate to Israel's agricultural lifestyle. God connected all of these feasts to harvest. In his doing so, we can find a picture detailing his plan to grow his kingdom throughout the entire world.

Passover

Passover, which comes in the spring, was the first national religious feast of the Hebrew people, both on their calendar and in their history. This may be confusing since the Jewish New Year, which we would assume to be the first festival, usually falls in September. But that event marks the traditional beginning of the fiscal or agricultural year, just like we might informally measure years by the start of school in September. On Israel's religious calendar, Passover occurs in the month of Nisan, which Scripture names as the first month.

Passover also was the first feast in Israeli history, celebrating God's dramatic redemption of the Hebrew people from bondage in Egypt, as recorded in the book of Exodus. As you recall, God poured out plague after plague on the Egyptians: afflicting them with physical maladies, ruining crops, killing cattle. Egypt's prosperity crumbled, yet the Hebrew people were spared. Still, Pharaoh refused to free the Israelites. The tenth plague—the final one—took the lives of firstborn sons throughout Egypt.

Israelites were not automatically spared this calamity. Rather, "God tempered his final judgment on Egypt with mercy and perfect provision—the substitution of a life for a life."[2] Exodus 12 records that God required every Israelite man to kill a lamb and paint the blood on the side posts and upper doorpost of his home. God said, "The blood will be a sign for you on the houses where you are; and when I see the blood, I will *pass over* you. No destructive plague will touch you when I strike Egypt" (Exodus 12:13, italics added). Thus, we get the name—*Passover.*

The word used in the original language is not the common Hebrew verb *a-bhar* or *ga-bhar*, which carries the idea of stepping or leaping over something to avoid contact. Rather, it is the verb *pasah*, which yields the noun *pesah*, translated "Passover." Messianic Jewish writers, Ceil and Moishe Rosen, citing other scholars, see no connection to any other Hebrew word but note that it resembles the Egyptian word *pesh*, which literally means "to spread wings over, especially to protect."[3]

God wanted his people to remember their deliverance as they re-enacted it through their annual Passover celebration. As the Rosens explain, "Even as we teach little children today through object lessons, Jehovah took everyday acts of seeing, hearing, smelling, tasting, and touching and made them his allies in teaching holy truths to his people."[4]

You can read the details for yourself in Exodus 12–13 and 34. The historical significance is obvious. The Hebrew people celebrated an actual event from their past, reflecting on a time when they saw tangible evidence of God's mercy and experienced his deliverance. This celebration also has prophetic significance with regard to the Messiah. The apostle Paul explained, "Christ, our Passover lamb, has been sacrificed" (1 Corinthians 5:7). He was referring to Jesus Christ, shedding his blood so God's judgment would *pass over* anyone who would humbly accept that substitution.

In a prophetic sense, Passover foreshadowed Christ's crucifixion. The Feast of Unleavened Bread, which accompanied Passover, requiring all Israelites to refrain from using yeast or any kind of leavening, reflected the removal of sin and the process of sanctification in the believer's life. And the Feast of Firstfruits, which also accompanied this celebration, looked forward to Christ's resurrection, as indicated by the apostle Paul, who wrote, "Christ has indeed been raised from the dead, the firstfruits of those who have fallen asleep" (1 Corinthians 15:20).

The Significance of "Firstfruits"

The Feast of Firstfruits provides the agricultural link for Passover, for it corresponds to the annual springtime barley harvest. Hebrew law required priests to present a wave offering—to literally wave a portion of the first harvested grain as a symbolic sacrifice to the Lord (see Leviticus 23:9–14).

Alfred Edersheim tells us that, at the time of Christ, delegates from the Sanhedrin would walk outside Jerusalem to a previously selected field in the Kidron Valley. Accompanied by a great crowd, this delegation would publicly reap the "Passover sheaf," which became the wave offering on the following day. Jewish tradition required this sheaf to come from an ordinary field—not a garden or an orchard—from soil that had not been fertilized with manure nor artificially watered. Then, on the appropriate evening—the Passover Sabbath—just as the sun went down, three men would reap an appropriate amount of grain.

That barley was threshed to remove the grain from the stalks. It was cooked in a perforated pan, so each grain would be touched by fire. Finally, it was exposed to the wind. Then it was ground into flour, part of which was mixed with oil and frankincense. The following day, the priest waved that mixture before the altar and then removed a handful for burning. This sacrifice, offered on the second day of Passover, accompanied a burnt offering of a year-old lamb and appropriate meat and drink offerings. All of this was required before Israelites could use or sell fresh barley.[5]

Edersheim believes this reaping occurred, in the story of Christ's crucifixion, at the same time as Jesus' burial, and the wave offering occurred with his resurrection. Regardless of the timing, it is true that Jesus used the same type of agrarian imagery to describe his upcoming death and resurrection. "Unless a kernel of wheat falls to the ground and dies," he told his disciples, "it remains only a single seed. But if it dies, it produces many seeds" (John 12:23–24). Thus, Passover and its accompanying ritual, which honored the Lord with the harvest's firstfruits, are realized in Christ's sacrificial death and victorious resurrection. This is the starting point for growing God's kingdom.

Pentecost

In Greek, the name *Pentecost* recognizes that this next feast came fifty days after Passover. The Hebrew people called it the Feast of Weeks, honoring the seven full weeks that fall between Passover and Pentecost. This means Pentecost falls in late spring or early summer, coinciding with the wheat harvest. Victor Buksbazen, as well as other scholars, concludes that it may have been the most popular Hebrew festival, for it came "when the cloudless skies of the Promised Land are blue and benign, the weather caressingly warm, and generally unmarred by the scorching desert wind."[6]

That is why so many people were in Jerusalem for the Feast of Pentecost described in Acts 2. The varying costumes and the cacophony of languages reflected their nationalities. But God interrupted the normal sequence of events for these travelers. Jesus' followers erupted into the streets, giving the message of salvation in varying languages "as the Spirit enabled them" (Acts 2:4). All those people heard the gospel in their own languages. Peter called them to repentance, and about 3,000 people responded and were baptized.

The timing was not a mere coincidence. According to Jewish tradition, Pentecost marked the anniversary of their receiving God's Law on Mount Sinai. In a very real sense, this holiday celebrated the birthday of Judaism—or some say the anniversary of the Hebrew nation's marriage to God. Looking through New Testament eyes, we see Pentecost marking the church's birth. But in a real sense, Pentecost also celebrates the fulfillment of that original marriage, pictured in Exodus as a covenant between God and the Hebrew nation, through the introduction of the church as the "bride of Christ." It also provides the spiritual application for a Jewish celebration designed to thank God for harvest. Acts 2 records a spiritual harvest—a cross-cultural missions event, with people from forty-three different countries drawn to Jerusalem for the outpouring of God's Spirit. That was the starting place for the growth of the global church.

The Feast of Booths

The Feast of Booths, also called the Feast of Tabernacles, occurred in Tishri, the seventh month on the Jewish religious calendar. In keeping with the "law of sevens," Tishri contained more holy days than any other, with the Feast of Trumpets, the Day of Atonement, and the Feast of Booths.

God instructed his people to blow trumpets at the beginning of every month. But a special observance marked this seventh month, and the sound of the *shofar* became its distinctive trait. The trumpet issued a call to repentance and a reminder that God, who had been faithful to his people, also required them to be faithful to him. This holiday is celebrated now as *Rosh Hashanah*, literally meaning "head of the year." It marks the beginning of the fiscal or agricultural year, thus becoming the Jewish New Year, but it falls in the seventh month, on the scriptural calendar, as does Yom Kippur, the Day of Atonement. This event, with its inclusion of the "scapegoat" ceremony (see Leviticus 16), was an ominous, awesome day of redemption and making peace with God.

Then came the Feast of Booths, also called the Feast of Tabernacles. This seven-day event in the seventh month completed the holiday season. It is the calendar's most joyous, festive holiday, so that some authors note, "It is . . . noteworthy that God placed Yom Kippur before the Feast of Tabernacles, the season of joy. The children of Israel could only rejoice once they were redeemed and their sins forgiven. The Day of Atonement rises as a peak among the mountains of Israel's feasts—a peak that one must scale to experience true joy. For God could pour out his blessings of joy only upon a forgiven people."[7]

To celebrate the Feast of Booths, called *Sukkot* in Hebrew, Jewish people built temporary shelters of branches and leaves and lived in them for seven days. This re-enactment of their ancestors' wilderness wanderings reminded them of God's faithfulness. In contrast with the sorrowful nature of the Feast of Trumpets and the Day of Atonement, this celebration is often called "The Season of Our Rejoicing." Since it coincides with the year's final harvest, it is also called the Feast of Ingathering.

In our contemporary age, we may have difficulty understanding the centrality of harvest in the Hebrew mindset. Mitch and Zhava Glaser of Chosen People Ministries explained it like this:

> Ancient Israel's economy was agrarian. There was no industry; there were no office buildings. . . . The focal point of daily life revolved around the crops the people needed for sustenance. . . . If there is a food shortage today, we have many alternative sources for supplies. However, that was not so for the Hebrews. Each season's plentiful harvest brought a renewed sense of relief and thankfulness that children would not go hungry, for God had once more provided for his people. . . . Perhaps that is why the feast of Ingathering also came to be called "The Season of Our Joy." The agricultural year was at an end, the crops were gathered into the storehouses. The work was done, the harvest was over; and the joy that was unleashed at the end of the long, hard labor found the perfect outlet for expression.[8]

The Global Feast

Based on this theme of bountiful harvest, it is interesting that Scripture links Sukkot with God's concern for those who are not yet included among his people. This emphasis reflects the Jewish understanding of their mission to grow God's kingdom, not just among Jews, but also among Gentiles. A few examples follow.

Solomon's Prayer to Dedicate the Temple

Solomon's dedication of the temple in Jerusalem coincided with the Feast of Booths.[9] In that prayer, Solomon interceded for Gentiles. "As for the foreigner who does not belong to your people Israel," he said, "when he comes and prays toward this temple, then hear from heaven . . . and do whatever the foreigner asks of you, *so that all the peoples of the earth may know your name and fear you, as do your own people Israel*" (1 Kings 8:41–43, italics added). Solomon repeated his missionary request, concluding, "may these words of mine, which I have prayed before the Lord, be near to the Lord our God day and night . . . *so that all the peoples of the earth may know that the LORD is God and that there is no other*" (1 Kings 8:59–60, italics added).

A Prophetic Call to the Nations

Jewish literature wraps the Feast of Booths around Israel's scriptural responsibility to bring redemption to the world. Mitch and Zhava Glaser believe the Israelites offered sacrifices during this celebration for other ethnic groups. They sought God's blessing so other nations could experience salvation and know the blessing of bountiful harvest, which comes only through obeying God's Word.[10]

The Israelites' understanding of their global mission had its root in Scripture, beginning with God's covenant with Abraham through which Hebrew people gained identity. God told Abraham that through his descendents, all the world's peoples would be blessed (see Genesis 12:1–3). That was a foreshadowing of the Messiah, born through Abraham's descendents to offer redemption to every ethnic group.

Furthermore, God gave Israel a two-fold responsibility. First, Israel was to serve as an expression of God's character.

Exodus 19:4–6 records God's admonition that Israel was to become "a kingdom of priests and a holy nation." Again in Isaiah 43:10, God specifically addresses Israel saying, "You are my witnessess." He repeats that in Isaiah 43:12 and again in Isaiah 44:8.

Second, their priestly mission encompassed the entire world. Psalm 67, for instance, opens with a request for God's blessing. But the request goes beyond a desire for personal welfare. Its purpose is so "your ways may be known on earth, your salvation among all nations" (verse 2). The passage describes the author's desire for all nations to come under God's dominion, learning to praise him as Lord. Isaiah 49:1 calls "distant nations" to attention, noting that Israel is God's servant, but adding, "It is too small a thing for you to be my servant to restore the tribes of Jacob and bring back those of Israel I have kept. I will also make you a light for the Gentiles, that you may bring my salvation to the ends of the earth" (Isaiah 49:6).

Scripture touches on that theme repeatedly. But specifically with the Feast of Booths, it looks forward to a time when all the world's nations will celebrate Sukkot. "Then the survivors from all the nations . . . will go up year after year to worship the King, the LORD Almighty, and to celebrate the Feast of Tabernacles" (Zechariah 14:16).

Refocus on Harvest

Clearly, these three Hebrew festivals build on one another: Passover, Pentecost, Feast of Booths. They foreshadow God's plan to grow his kingdom—Christ's sacrificial death and resurrection birthed the church that, like Israel, has a global mandate to take the good news of redemption and blessing to the whole world. (See Great Commission verses in Matthew

28:18–20; Mark 16:15–16; Luke 24:46–48; John 17:20–23.) Acts 1:8 particularly calls Jesus' followers to be his witnesses "in Jerusalem, and in all Judea and Samaria, and to the ends of the earth." The Greek does not imply a geographic ministry progression, first Jerusalem, then Judea, then Samaria, then the ends of the earth. Rather, it implies that Christ's followers are to be involved simultaneously in all four sectors.

In contemporary application, that means all local churches and individual Christians must find ways to be involved in concurrent ministry in their own culture, in similar cultures, and in cultures that are entirely different from their own. That can happen through personal contact with individuals, but it can also happen through praying, giving, and supporting those who go to other cultures to grow God's kingdom. This kind of ministry focus will happen naturally as we renew our understanding of the centrality of harvest. Most of us work nine-to-five jobs, or maybe eight-to-six or seven-to-seven jobs, earning money that we trade for things we need or want, including food. In an age when most of our meals come from the grocery store or the restaurant, we've lost touch with the necessity of harvest as reflected in the Jewish feasts.

Farmer, editor, and teacher Ben Logan, who grew up on a farm in Wisconsin in the 1920s and 1930s, fondly remembers one year when the weather stayed unusually warm, even into November. Then suddenly it turned deathly cold. The family had already harvested and stored their grain, but the vegetables and fruit remained in the garden and orchard. That was their sustenance for the long, harsh winter.

He recalls one long day of hard work, digging carrots, beets, and turnips, even as other family members brought potatoes from the fields. He picked the last green beans and lettuce, explaining, "The lettuce leaves were too big and would be bitter, but they were the last we would have for seven months."[11] He picked ground cherries, cabbage, and squash, then ran to the orchard to pick the last apples. All the while his mother was canning produce to store it for the winter.

Logan concludes, "That night, with the chores done and a fire roaring in the dining-room stove, the house was warm and steamy, filled with good earthy smells from orchard and garden. Except for some late corn still drying in the fields, harvest was over. We had lived another growing season in partnership with the land. Now the land's gifts were safely stored in the cellar, barns, granary, corncrib and haystacks. Suddenly it didn't matter that the bright days of Indian summer were over and that the ground would be frozen by morning."[12]

Israel's harvests looked a little different, but their importance was the same. Harvest meant survival. As God wrote Israel's history, he placed Israel's primary festivals at times of harvest. Similarly, he also inspired his prophet to use harvest terminology in describing the coming of the Messiah. In foretelling the birth and ministry of Christ, Isaiah wrote, "The people walking in darkness have seen a great light; on those living in the land of the shadow of death a light has dawned . . . *they rejoice before you as people rejoice at the harvest"* (Isaiah 9:2,3b, italics added).

That imagery demonstrates that, in a physical sense, harvest was the central focus of everyday life for the Hebrew people. We must mirror that in a spiritual sense. A harvest mentality must be central to everything we do.

Sow This Book into Your Life

1.   Church history records the experience of John Knox, a Scottish reformer in the sixteenth century. Knox prayed a heartfelt request to God: "Give me Scotland," he said, "*or*

I will die." In essence, he expressed a desire for spiritual harvest that was so strong, he felt he would die if it didn't happen. Knox had a clear understanding that spiritual harvest is crucial for survival. It was his primary—perhaps even solitary—goal. And by the end of his lifetime, Scotland had undergone widespread reform.

Examine your heart carefully and, with brutal honesty, fill in the blank for yourself: "Lord, give me _____, or I will die."

Is your request related to harvest? Is harvest the focus of your life? Or is it just a peripheral issue? Explain your answer.

_____

_____

What about your church? Here's a circle. Put a mark on the circle to describe where harvest fits into your church's overall goals. Is it at the center of everything your church does? Or is it a peripheral issue? Explain your answer.

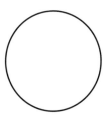

_____

_____

_____

P   A   R   A

2. A senior pastor from a church in Virginia Beach, Virginia, told me his church has "set God's last command as our first priority." He refers to the "Great Commission" verses—the last command that Jesus gave to his followers before he ascended into heaven. What was that command? (If you need help, look up Matthew 28:18–20; Mark 16:15–16; Luke 24:46–48; John 17:20–23; Acts 1:8.)

It appears that harvest is central to this congregation's understanding of their reason for existence. Based on your answer to question number one, what immediate steps can you and/or your church take to refocus on harvest?

_____

_____

In preparation for chapter 5, read:

Galatians 6:7–10

2 Corinthians 9:6–11

Genesis 8:18–22

chapter 5 < what Is harvest?

D   an Fouts, outstanding quarterback for the San Diego
        Chargers from 1973 through 1987, refers to a game
        that occurred early in his professional career. It was
Don Coryell's first year as head coach, and he had put together
an impressive staff that included Jim Hanifan, Joe Gibbs, and
Ernie Zambese. With two minutes left in the first half, Fouts
went to the sideline to discuss a crucial play.

Fouts expected Coryell to tell him what to do. Instead, the
assistants overwhelmed him with information. Based on data
relayed by Gibbs and Zambese, Hanifan told him, "On the
next play, we're going to run eight-forty-four wide. You want
to look at the weak safety, and if the weak safety stays in the
middle, try to hit Charlie Joiner on the post. Now, if the weak
safety hangs to the weak side, then try to hit Kellan Winslow
over the middle, and then there's J.J. (John Jefferson), who's
running a corner. Now, if the linebackers drop back too far,
then dump it off to Chuck Muncie underneath. . . ."

The assistants all talked at once, but Coryell didn't say a
word.

Fouts explains, "I was restrapping my helmet, thinking,
*Here's the most innovative offensive coach in football, and I
haven't heard a word from him."* Then Coryell pulled Fouts'
jersey to get his attention. The wise coach instructed his young
quarterback, "Just throw to J.J."

Discussion ended.[1]

Back to Basics

We've all seen occasions when someone needed to strip away extraneous stuff and get back to basics. We've already looked at some scriptural basics related to God's part in harvest. He is Lord of the land, Lord of time, and Lord of harvest. We transition now to look at the scriptural basics related to our part in the process that will grow his kingdom.

I heard about a man who adopted an overgrown vacant lot in an inner city. With great personal sacrifice and care, he lovingly turned that eyesore into a colorful garden. One day, as he was cultivating flowers and pulling weeds, someone parked a car beside his paradise and came to admire his work.

"God sure did a good job of creating this beauty, didn't he?" the visitor asked.

The gardener unfolded himself from a crouch. Placing his hands on his hips, he squinted at the guest. "Sure," he said. "God did a great job. But you should have seen this place when he was tending it by himself."

God alone is Lord of everything involved in the harvest, but for a reason only he knows, he invites us to participate in his project. We get into trouble when we try to take his place, assuming rights of ownership. We also leave him with a messy, unproductive vacant lot when we neglect to steward his land, his time, and his harvest into fruitfulness.

Stewardship responsibility is the underlying theme of harvest, and it is as true in the spiritual realm as it is in the physical. Understanding our responsibilities, then, requires that we go back to the basics of farming.

You Reap What You Sow

Ultimately, your harvest will be defined by the kinds of seeds you plant. If you plant tomatoes, you will get tomatoes. Scripture makes a spiritual application, saying that God will not be mocked; the principles he built into the physical world generally prove true in the spiritual realm. Thus, a person who "sows to please his sinful nature, from that nature will reap destruction; the one who sows to please the Spirit . . . will reap eternal life" (Galatians 6:7–8). The passage obviously applies to the individual, but I see an application for churches as well.

It is clear in agriculture. If you plant lettuce, you'll get lettuce. If you plant barley, you will get barley. And if you plant tobacco, you will get tobacco. Unfortunately, many churches thought they were sowing a gainful harvest, and it turned out to be spiritual tobacco. Let me explain.

Tobacco requires a lot of energy and resources. Ben Logan, who grew up on a farm in the 1920s and '30s, explains that tobacco is a cash crop, but it is also a "back breaker—hard on the land, hard on people," and demanding time when other crops also need attention. "Almost everything about tobacco, except smoking it, meant working with your back bent into a circle," he adds. "We didn't like tobacco much," Logan writes. "It took a lot out of the soil, and left only the stalks . . . but the real richness of the crop had gone to market to be burned into ashes."

Logan notes, "Many a farm went slowly to ruin . . . because of tobacco. . . . The vicious circle of land misuse went on until it broke the farm and its people. In the end, the buildings were half falling, the dairy cattle thin, the cornfields full of nubbins, and the people worn out and bent into a permanent circle."

His own father slowly built up dairy herds and concentrated on other crops, so he could quit growing tobacco. Logan concludes, "Tobacco had been an alien to us. I don't think it had anything to do with whether or not it was right to smoke. . . . But it may have had something to do with a larger, more subtle morality. Other crops completed the cycle from growth to new growth with enough of the crop going back to the land in manure or waste to keep the soil healthy. Other crops worked with the land, building it. Tobacco used up the land." [2]

Choose Your Seed Wisely

Patrick Johnstone's global prayer guide, *Operation World*, tells us that 68 percent of Australia's population claim to be Christian. Still, it reports, the culture follows the Western ideals of "secularism and a pursuit of pleasure and wealth."[3] This is reflected in an e-mail I received from a pastor who ministers primarily among Australia's immigrant populations. He wrote, "Most of these Christian migrants come to Australia for their children's education and with the mindset of having a good life here (Australia is called the 'lucky' country)." He added, "There are a handful of our members who are fervent and passionate but the great majority are lukewarm."

These statements characterize the struggle of Christian churches in the affluent West. Many issues contribute to the tendency for Christians to lose sight of the mandate to grow God's kingdom. Given that tendency, therefore, church leaders must be very careful when they choose the seed they sow into their congregations.

Christian statistics guru George Barna tells us that, in the United States, 84 percent of American pastors say their churches are "evangelistic." Yet Barna notes, "These figures are perplexing in light of the fact that the average weekly adult attendance reported by pastors actually decreased by 9 percent. . . . This coincides with a 15 percent drop in the average annual church operating budget."[4] Furthermore, Barna says that among Americans who claim to be "born again" only 60 percent could correctly identify at least one legitimate definition of the term "gospel."[5]

These figures imply that pastors and leaders may be sowing the spiritual equivalent of tobacco seeds. They intentionally or unintentionally plant the idea that the church exists for itself. Barna was asked to define trends that he sees among churches that are not making disciples. The primary trend, he said, is that they are "overly concerned about keeping happy." He adds, "Those churches also are too focused on comfort. . . .When we become internally comfortable, we create a system that facilitates or fosters the absence of commitment" to engaging and evangelizing the surrounding culture.[6]

Granted, that kind of spiritual misunderstanding can take root in a Christian fellowship, even if it is not upheld and taught by church leaders. But, when church leaders foster that kind of spiritual environment in their congregations, they are sowing the spiritual equivalent of tobacco seed. The congregation becomes self-seeking, spending vast amounts of money and re-sources on programs and projects that benefit only themselves. Such a church may have some community involvement, but for the most part, its people fellowship in a "holy huddle," rarely moving beyond the familiar group of Christians who occupy their time and absorb their capital.

That may sound like a harsh assessment, but statistics like those provided by Barna support this view. Spiritual tobacco seed yields a harvest of sorts, but it is a harvest that sees only short-term gain. The church growth that results from sowing this kind of seed may seem like a cash crop, even yielding a variety of flourishing church programs and big budget building programs, but, like crops of tobacco, those churches require lots of work. They devour the time of their leaders. They erode the surrounding community and culture. In the long-term, the repeated sowing of self-serving seed will rob churches of the very nutrients they need to survive and thrive.

Patrick Johnstone, in *Operation World*, describes the harvest that churches are reaping in the United States as the result of the inappropriate sowing of spiritual tobacco seed. "The spiritual heritage of the USA is being eroded," he explains. "The Christian Church is not impacting the nation as it should. The USA needs revival, yet the word 'revival' has been debased to mean slick, mass evangelism and theatrics. The need of the hour is a true revival with conviction of sin, repentance and an outpouring of the Holy Spirit."[7]

This trend is not limited to the United States. *Operation World* also notes, "The last 250 years have been years of worldwide advance for the gospel but, conversely, decline in Europe." The authors list eight major people-groups in Europe with very strong Christian traditions but very few contemporary evangelical believers. They explain, "Great swathes of Western Europe are truly post-Christian with a small, 'irrelevant,' committed Christian remnant, and need to be evangelized again—for example, North Germany, parts of Sweden, rural England and Wales, and much of France. Many of these areas have not had much meaningful exposure to biblical Christianity for several generations."[8]

These comments indicate a cultural slide away from Christianity. Paul Borthwick, a long-time minister of missions, believes this loss of impact on our culture has come about because "we have become convinced that the mission of the church is to make sure that Christians are happy and content. We focus on our own fellowship and doctrinal purity, often at the expense of interaction with the world. As a result, we render the church virtually irrelevant to the issues of our world." He adds, "Although most of us believe . . . that the gospel has the power to change lives and therefore societies . . . we fail to act on it." He quotes Luis Palau, who tells us that, in the U.S., there is "little enthusiasm for evangelism. Political action, yes. Public protest, yes. Open and vigorous soul-winning, no."[9]

That failure comes from the seed we have sown. We have planted spiritual tobacco seed, and we are reaping a bitter harvest. Our ability to change the statistics depends on getting back to the basic agricultural understanding that we will reap what we sow. We must choose our seeds more wisely.

We will look at this more carefully later. For now, let us say we should be sowing a proper view of God, of ourselves, and of our role in growing his kingdom. Borthwick asks six questions, believing our intellectual responses—and our ability to integrate them into our lifestyles—will alter our understanding of the role of individual Christians and of their local churches in the world at large.

- Who is Jesus?
- Do I believe in heaven?
- Do I believe in hell?
- Does Christianity matter?
- Do I believe that God wants to use my life?
- Whose agenda will I live by?

I challenge you to answer those kinds of questions biblically within your congregation. Giving scriptural responses to those issues, and others like them, will provide good seed—the kind of seed that will yield long-term results of a productive global harvest. Keep away from the tobacco seed, and invest in this kind of seed instead.

P A R A

Plant a Little, Harvest a Little

The size of your harvest depends greatly on the amount of seed you plant. That is obvious in the physical world, but it is also true in the spiritual realm. For example, in a passage related to cheerful and generous giving, the apostle Paul writes, "Whoever sows sparingly will reap sparingly, and whoever sows generously will also reap generously. Each man should give what he has decided in his heart to give, not reluctantly or under compulsion, for God loves a cheerful giver" (2 Corinthians 9:6–7).

If that is true at the individual level, it is also true at the corporate level. Generous churches reap generous harvests. Many pastors say if they could see the members' checkbooks, they could gauge spiritual commitment. It is also true of churches. A church that spends all of its money on itself reveals little commitment to growing Christ's kingdom. That church will reap a tiny harvest. In contrast, a church that gives wisely, but with an open hand and a generous heart, will reap a large harvest.

My area of expertise is cross-cultural missions. I suggest any church that wants a part in rewriting the future for people in other cultures should give at least 10 percent of its total budget to foreign missions, and then move to a higher percentage through Faith Promise Giving. In making Faith Promises, individuals in a congregation prayerfully consider the amount God wants them to give, over and above their tithe, usually to a specific project. This is an agreement between the individual and God—not between the individual and the church. They usually make a written pledge of some kind, and then trust God to give that amount to them, or help them earn it. They, in turn, pass it on as an offering.

As I have noted, however, I also believe the church has a responsibility to minister to the congregation, to the community and culture where the church is located, and to other cultures. Given that three-way breakdown, some churches may want to assign a third of their budget to each area. Other churches feel particularly called to give large amounts to a specific area of outreach. For instance, I know some that give up to 60 percent of their church budget to cross-cultural ministry.

Paul made it clear that "each man should give what he has decided in his heart to give, not reluctantly or under compulsion." (2 Corinthians 9:6–7). The same applies to churches. Each should give the amount decided before God. In making that decision, however, remember Paul's admonition: if you sow sparingly, you will reap sparingly.

Reaping Sprouts?

In considering the realities of spiritual harvest, we also need to examine the practice of harvesting sprouts. Perhaps you are familiar with alfalfa or bean sprouts, easily found at salad bars and used in sandwiches at many delicatessens. Sprouts are simply immature plants, harvested when they are still very young.

There are health benefits to eating spouts, for they contain huge amounts of essential nutrients. They burgeon with antioxidants that help fight disease. For instance, broccoli contains a natural cancer-fighting agent. But a one-ounce serving of broccoli sprouts can have as much of that agent as one-and-one-quarter pounds of cooked adult broccoli.[10] Sprouts also can be high in protein, chlorophyll, vitamins, minerals, enzymes, and other nutrients that support the human body.

Sprouts are tasty. They make for good eating, and they have the potential to improve the health of the one who eats them. But in the agricultural world, you either have to leave them in the ground to grow or eat them. At this level of maturity, they can't reproduce themselves.

In local churches, we often define and gauge harvest in terms of conversions. That is the spiritual equivalent of filling our barns with sprouts. In his classic book *Basic Christianity*, John R.W. Stott wrote, "The great privilege of the child of God is relationship; his great responsibility is growth. Everybody loves children, but nobody in his right mind wants them to stay in the nursery. The tragedy, however, is that many Christians, born again in Christ, never grow up."[11] Churches encourage that appalling eternal baby-hood when they fail to view harvest in terms of maturity.

Jesus didn't tell us to "go and make converts of all nations." He told us to "go and make disciples" (Matthew 28:19). Stott defines discipleship in terms of maturity, which includes scriptural knowledge and personal sanctification, but he says it doesn't stop there. We have a responsibility to remain in fellowship with God through continued confession, Bible study, and prayer, and to make lifestyle choices that reflect his character.

We also have responsibility to interact with the church and with the world. He explains, "The Christian life is a family affair, in which the children enjoy fellowship with their Father and with each other. But let it not for one moment be thought that this exhausts the Christian's responsibilities. . . . The Christian church has a noble record of philanthropic work for the needy and neglected people. . . . Still today all over the world the followers of Christ are seeking in his name to alleviate suffering and distress. Yet an enormous amount of work is waiting to be done."[12] Stott stresses that the particular way in which Christians are to influence the world is through evangelism.

Missions researcher James Engel, with his writing partner H. Wilbur Norton, offers similar wisdom when he outlines a scale to gauge "The Spiritual-Decision Process." The scale begins on the minus side with "Awareness of Supreme Being, but No Effective Knowledge of the Gospel." It advances through various stages of acceptance of the gospel and recognition and confession of sin. Then it hits "Regeneration." Most of us would stop there, but for Engel, that is just a little past the halfway point on the continuum. There are still six steps in the process:

- Post-Decision Evaluation
- Incorporation into the Body
- Conceptual and Behavioral Growth
- Communion with God
- Stewardship
- Reproduction[13]

As Engel and Norton remind us, "New life does not stop . . . with regeneration."[14] The goal for every believer should be to imitate God's character and fulfill his desires. His Word clearly says his primary desire is to have a kingdom of worshippers, and that kingdom is to spread out all over the world, taking in every ethnic group and every culture. Every Christian is responsible for discovering how God wants him to participate in that great endeavor. Every local church is responsible for creating an environment for the individual believer to be part of a harvest team.

It all begins with a proper view of harvest. We have to quit storing up sprouts and start cultivating mature and fruitful plants.

Harvest Is a Process

Finally, as Engel and Norton imply, spiritual harvest is a process. Effective communication of the gospel is not limited to the task of bringing people to salvation. Communicating the gospel means meeting a person or a group of people wherever they are on the continuum of "The Spiritual-Decision Process," and moving them toward the final goal of maturity and reproduction.[15]

Harvest is an event, but it is also a process. In the physical world, harvest doesn't happen in a vacuum. It is the end of a process that began many months beforehand. In the biblical world, harvest also launched the next agricultural season, providing seeds for the following year's crop. Paradoxically, it is both an end and a beginning.

That is the theme for the rest of this book. We intend to dissect various parts of the agricultural cycle and glean spiritual applications to help churches through the process of helping to grow God's kingdom. Our goal is the restoration of a biblical harvest paradigm within the church. So we will look at seven steps in the harvest continuum:

- Clearing the land
- Preparing the soil
- Matching the seed to the soil
- Sowing the seed
- Cultivating the crop
- Harvesting the crop
- Preparing it for future use

In the real world, this process usually is not tied up in an orderly little package. Ben Logan describes the agricultural environment like this: "There is no neat and easy way to tell the story of a farm. A farm is a process, where everything is related, everything happening at once." He adds, "Years were hard to separate on a farm. A year is an arbitrary, calendar thing. Our lives revolved around the seasons." Spring represented new life. Summer was heat and hard work. Fall was the end of the growing season and the burst of color. Winter was the "in-between time." Then, as if by magic, spring arrived again, and the process started all over.[16]

After the great flood, God promised that kind of progression. When Noah built an altar to the Lord and sacrificed burnt offerings on it, Scripture tells us the aroma pleased God. In response, God said to Himself, "Never again will I curse the ground because of man." The Lord promised, "As long as the earth endures, seedtime and harvest, cold and heat, summer and winter, day and night will never cease" (Genesis 8:21–22). Then he made a covenant with Noah and hung the rainbow in the sky as a reminder of that on-going commitment.

God's description of seasons can be paraphrased like this: "As sure as there is night and day, winter and summer, there will be seed-time and harvest." The agricultural cycle reflects God's character. Planting and harvest are within his nature. It's true physically and spiritually. This is how God intends to grow his kingdom—through the on-going process of "seed-time and harvest." He has a place for us at every stage in the process, which will fulfill his desire to extend his harvest field over the whole earth.

Sow This Book into Your Life

Several pastors and church leaders responded to our series of questions about spiritual harvest. Their revealing answers helped us formulate the concepts that undergird this work.

A long-time pastor of a church in Fort Wayne, Indiana, for instance, told me he believes God builds churches for four specific purposes: fellowship, instruction, worship, and evangelism. Furthermore, harvest should be the "first priority of a mature body of believers." That agrees with the information presented in Chapter 5. It also determines the kind and amount of seed that an individual or a church will sow into the harvest process.

When I asked how he would determine whether his church is a harvest church, this pastor suggested three factors:

- How much of the church's income is invested in harvest?

- How much of the church's time is devoted to harvest?

- How many from the congregation are personally involved in harvest?

By contrast, an administrator from another church in Kansas City, Missouri, told us her church has a three-fold mission—to reach the lost; to restore people to Christ-like maturity; and to release people into ministry. But for the last question, she gave a brutally honest answer. To the question "Would you call your church a harvest church?" she responded, "By all indications, this is not our primary area of emphasis. Although it is in our mission statement, the money and volunteers devoted to evangelism would indicate that it is not one of our priorities."

Both of these responses incorporate the idea that money, time, and personal involvement are legitimate first-steps in evaluating whether your church leadership team and your congregation have truly grasped the centrality of harvest. It is not just one of many things to be considered in planning your church calendar; it is the crucial issue that should guide every decision for an individual Christian or a corporate body of believers.

Because of this, we challenge you to prayerfully ask these questions:

- Is harvest my personal priority?
- Is harvest the priority of my church leadership team?
- Is my church a harvest church?

Then take a look at your investment of time and money, and if you are discussing this for application to a church, look also at the investment of personnel and volunteers. Record what you find there.

_____

_____

_____

1. Do your findings support your initial conclusions?

_____

_____

2. What do you need to change?

_____

_____

3. How will you make it happen?

_____

_____

A senior pastor of a church in Wyckoff, New Jersey, noted that in measuring the success of his church's ministry outreach, both in the local community and in cultures on the other side of the world, he asks himself four questions. Three were general evaluation questions that you would expect anyone to ask. But the fourth was very telling. This pastor asks himself, "Is the devil mad" as the result of what is happening at his church? I hope that, when you apply that question to your church, you can answer as he did: "Absolutely."

In preparation for chapter 6, read:

Daniel 6:1–10

Daniel 9:1–19

Ephesians 6:12

chapter 6 < clearing the land

I remember with incredible clarity the day I watched the Berlin Wall disappear. When I lived and ministered in Germany, I frequently traveled through Checkpoint Charlie, answering questions and submitting to searches of my person and my vehicle as I drove between West and East Berlin. I knew the Wall's inconveniences. For me, and for many others, the Berlin Wall was the world's most visible symbol of communism's abject cruelty.

Communism's European martyrs numbered in the millions. Christians were harassed and imprisoned. Their Bibles and literature were confiscated. Their church meetings were raided. Richard Wurmbrand, spokesman for persecuted Christians behind the Iron Curtain, described "unspeakable tortures borne by Christians."

Despite all this, they triumphed, because they recognized the true identity of their enemy and the true source of their power. Wurmbrand wrote, "We wrestle not against flesh and blood, but against the principalities and powers of evil. We saw that communism is not from men but from the devil. It is a spiritual force—a force of evil—and can only be countered by a greater spiritual force, the Spirit of God."[1]

In November of 1989, the dismantling of the Berlin Wall symbolized the sweeping changes that were coming to this region. I sat in my living room and watched this momentous event on TV. I saw a boy about ten years old whom I will call "Peter," a popular German name. He crawled from his father's shoulders to join the revelers atop the wall. Camera lights illuminated his blond hair dancing in the damp, chilly breeze. Peter took a chisel in his left hand and a hammer in his right. Sparks leaped around his hands as metal struck metal, and Peter began to peck away at the wall, perhaps claiming his own souvenir of the event.

In that incredible moment, the Holy Spirit spoke to me. "This boy represents the thousands of people who have chipped away at this wall for years," he said. "They have prayed, and this is my answer."

Clearing the Land

Some people would express this victory in military terms, saying the prayer warriors who brought down that wall were "tearing down Satan's strongholds." But in agricultural language, I would say they were "clearing the land."

Ruth spent some of her growing-up years on an agricultural training settlement in Zambia. Her father, assigned by his missions organization to work under the Zambian government, kept the settlement running and taught necessary skills for national farmers to make an adequate living and provide for their families.

Each participant received five acres of thick forest. The first step was to clear the land. Two huge bulldozers would drive in tandem, a large iron chain stretched between, toppling a wide swath of trees. Zambian families chopped up the wood and burned it in tiny clay huts, making charcoal to sell at market. Then they began digging and pulling out large roots and rocks. It took a lot of work and time, but the land, once densely forested so that sunlight did not reach it and where hard rocks stifled undergrowth, was made arable and fruitful. (See

"Sow This Book into Your Life" at the end of this chapter for more agricultural principles related to clearing the land.)

That is exactly what those prayer warriors accomplished with the fall of communism in Europe. By God's grace, they knocked down and chopped up the things that obstructed kingdom growth but not without a huge investment of time and energy. They were faithful. They partnered with him through prayer and intercession, and in the process, they participated in an event that only God could accomplish.

Why Pray?

As we have already noted in this book, God is the Lord of the land. He is the Lord of time, and he is the Lord of the harvest. He is, in fact, Lord of everything. Scripture clearly tells us that salvation is the result of his intervention in our lives through grace, and nothing can be added to bring redemption (Ephesians 2:8–9); no one comes to the Father except through Jesus (John 14:6); and no one can come to Jesus unless the Father draws him or her (John 6:44).

We could assume that God will take care of the whole harvest, from beginning to end, leaving no real reason for individuals to participate. Based on that assumption, if we pray at all, we might imitate a little girl whose grandfather asked her to say grace at the table. Holding his hand, she bowed her head and began to say, "A . . . B . . . C . . . D." Her grandfather stopped her and asked, "Sweetie, what are you doing?" She replied, "I'm praying. I just give God the letters and let him spell whatever he wants to."

It is a cute story that some have used to illustrate complete trust in God's plan. Adults who imitate that kind of intercession, however, have fallen prey to faulty logic. Brother Andrew, who ministers primarily in regions that are hostile to the gospel, has a name for that kind of reasoning. He calls it *Christian fatalism*, noting that it fits more comfortably into Islam or Hinduism or Buddhism than into true, biblical Christianity. Brother Andrew believes that people who ascribe to that philosophy are "steeped in a false doctrine that has infected the thinking of an alarming number of Christians in our time." He writes, "There is . . . no place for fatalism in Christianity. Quite the opposite!"

Brother Andrew adds that, in creating us in his own image, God gave to mankind "the privilege of choosing how our lives (and our world) will turn out. And those of us who know God are elevated to a stunning position within this framework: we become God's partners and collaborators in writing the story of mankind. Not only that, but we are empowered to challenge the powers of evil that have been at war with God since the beginning of time. We can, through our own faith and our prayers, lift the world off its hinges—*if only we will!*"[2]

What does that mean? It means that God created man in his image, and as recorded in Genesis, he gave man a specific destiny and purpose: to fill, subdue, and have dominion over the earth. We were intended to be God's representatives, enforcing his will in the realm that he placed under our care.

Andrew Murray's classic work *With Christ in the School of Prayer* explains what happens when an earthly king sends a representative to some other part of the world. He gives that ambassador a certain level of authority, and he takes the ambassador's advice regarding what actions are necessary to accomplish the king's desires and intentions. Murray notes, "If the sovereign . . . doesn't approve of the policy, he replaces the representative with someone who better understands his desires for the empire. But as long as the representative is trusted, his advice is carried out."

In serving as ambassador for the King of Kings, Murray explains, man was to have similar power. "On his advice and at his request, heaven was to have bestowed its blessing on earth. His prayer was to have been the natural channel through which the Lord in heaven and man, as lord of this world, communicated. The destinies of the world were given into the power of the wishes, the will, and the prayers of man."[3]

When Adam and Eve sinned, they brought a curse on the very world they were supposed to rule for God's glory. But, writes Murray, "prayer still remains what it would have been if man had never fallen: the proof of man's Godlikeness, the vehicle of his communication with the Father, and the power that is allowed to hold the hand that holds the destinies of the universe. . . . What sin destroyed, grace has restored."[4]

Murray concludes, "As God's image-bearer and representative on earth, redeemed man has the power to determine the history of this earth through his prayers. Man was created and then redeemed to pray, and by his prayer to have dominion."[5] This understanding is crucial at every stage of harvest. When we are in the stage of clearing the land, whether we are looking for harvest in the life of an individual loved one, in our community, or in a people group on the other side of the world, prayer is the only tool that will successfully uproot what stands in the way of God's harvest.

God's sovereignty is unquestionable, but it doesn't release us from the obligation to pray. Rather, it should undergird our confidence to pray, because we know our petitions aren't futile. The sovereign God who hears them is able to do "immeasurably more than all we ask or imagine" (Ephesians 3:20).

P A R A

A Biblical Example

The Bible gives several examples of people who rested in God's sovereignty yet felt compelled to partner with him through prayer. One example is Daniel, who is described as being from Hebrew nobility "without any physical defect, handsome, showing aptitude for every kind of learning, well informed, quick to understand, and qualified to serve in the king's palace" (Daniel 1:4). Daniel showed special promise, but he also showed incredible resolve as a youth. Determining to follow Jehovah, he refused to succumb to the godless traditions of the foreign culture that surrounded him, even in matters of diet. God honored him, and he rose to prominence in Babylon.

Even in exile, Daniel developed a lifestyle of prayer. Perhaps the most widely known story of Daniel's life comes from his experience in the lion's den when God shut the mouths of those big cats, and Daniel escaped unscathed. But maybe you've forgotten why Daniel was there in the first place.

Because some officials and authorities envied Daniel's political power, they sought to undermine his position with the king. Scripture says they began to watch Daniel, looking for some grounds to bring charges against him. But, "they could find no corruption in him, because he was trustworthy and neither corrupt nor negligent." Finally they gave up. "We will never find any basis for charges against this man Daniel unless it has something to do with the law of his God," they said (Daniel 6:4–5).

Appealing to the king's ego, they sneakily tricked their ruler into establishing a thirty-day period wherein every king-dom resident would be required to worship the king or meet the lions. Even in the face of that threat, Daniel refused to give up the privilege of intercession. Scripture says, "Now when Daniel learned that the decree had been published, he went home to his upstairs room where the windows opened toward Jerusalem. Three times a day he got down on his knees and prayed, giving thanks to his God, just as he had done before" (Daniel 6:10).

Daniel refused to be intimidated into giving up the activities that he considered to be crucial. He was willing to face the lions rather than quit praying, and God honored that commitment by delivering him.

That same commitment showed up later in Daniel's life. As he read Jeremiah's prophecies, he understood the exact timing of Israel's deliverance from exile. We know Daniel trusted God's sovereignty. Now he also had God's prophetic promise of liberty. For most of us, that would have been reason to quit praying and begin celebrating, but that's not what Daniel did. Instead, he "turned to the Lord God and pleaded with him in prayer and petition, in fasting, and in sackcloth and ashes" (Daniel 9:3). He continued confessing the Israelites' sins and seeking God's mercy, so he could see God glorified in the restoration of his people.

Similarly, we have God's promise that he doesn't want anyone to perish, but he wants everyone to come to repentance (2 Peter 3:9). We also have his prophecy that ensures the success of global harvest, since we know that people of every tribe, tongue, and nation will be gathered before his eternal throne (Revelation 5:9 and 7:9).

So why should we pray? Because of what we learn from Daniel. As author Derek Prince explained, "The prophecies and promises of God's Word are never an excuse to cease praying. On the contrary, they are intended to provoke us to pray with increased earnestness and understanding. God reveals to us the purposes which he is working out, not that we may be passive spectators on the sidelines of history, but that we may personally identify ourselves with his purposes and, thus, become actively involved in their fulfillment."[6]

For Whom Should We Pray?

There is a church in Honolulu, Hawaii, that has grown by fifteen hundred members each year for the last five years and now has ten thousand people in attendance at weekend services and is still growing. The senior pastor notes that more than 70 percent of the growth has come through conversions rather than transfer or biological growth. Perhaps this success rests in his basic definition of evangelism, which is "simply gathering in the spoils previously won in prayer."

Most of us agree that prayer is a critical factor in accomplishing anything that has eternal significance. If you are like me, you have a fairly lengthy prayer list that includes many different requests. Since this book primarily deals with harvest, let's examine how a harvest mindset should affect our prayer lists.

Evangelism can be broken down into three types: E1, E2, and E3 evangelism. Simply put, E1 evangelism targets those in our own culture (perhaps unsaved family or friends, or even community leaders, neighbors, or acquaintances). The next level, E2 evangelism, targets those in cultures similar to our own (for instance, those who live in other Western nations). And E3 evangelism targets those who live in cultures that are entirely different from ours.

God wants every local church and every individual believer to have some type of involvement in all three sectors. The most basic contribution comes in prayer.

E1 Praying

Begin with your family, your friends, and your community. Count how many unsaved people you pray for on a regular basis, then take that number before God and ask him if there are more individuals or groups he wants you to add to that list.

Don't forget to pray for revival in your own nation. Those who study revival movements tell us revivals always follow extensive prayer efforts. In *Revival Fire* Wesley Duewel notes, "When we study the history of God's work on earth, we will always find faithful praying saints, often hidden, holding on before him in prayer, pleading for God to revive his people. Always there were people—often many—who in the privacy of their hearts cried out to God over and over."[7]

Duewel gives many examples, including that of Evan Roberts, a young Welshman who was "spiritually responsive his entire life." Even as a child, Roberts read his Bible, prayed, and memorized hymns. He was known to lead kiddie church services, preaching to neighborhood children. From the time he turned thirteen, Roberts "prayed continually for God to fill him with the Holy Spirit and to send revival to Wales." Often he preferred praying to eating or sleeping.

Finally, after thirteen years of praying, God answered Roberts' in a mighty way. At the nine o'clock church service on a Sunday morning, God filled Roberts with his Holy Spirit, Duewel tells us. Within a matter of days, national revival began as well. Roberts began praying for a hundred thousand souls to be saved as a result of that revival, and God gave him the confident assurance that it would happen. Evan Roberts was used mightily by God as an instrument to bring revival to Wales. Why? Because he was willing to pray.[8]

E2 and E3 Praying

At AIMS, we have seen God answer prayer more times than we can count. Let me share one example.

AIMS has an eight-year history of working with the Evangelical Churches Fellowship of Ethiopia (ECFE), which represents 97 percent of that country's evangelical believers. In December of 2000, the ECFE invited AIMS to do our first-ever multi-track training event overseas. One track was specifically to address HIV/AIDS. According to statistics provided by the UN and the World Health Organization, 40 million people in the world have HIV, and about 10 percent of them live in Ethiopia. Furthermore, Ethiopia is home to about 1.2 million AIDS orphans. The Ethiopian Church views this an opportunity for ministry, and they asked AIMS to provide training to help them.

This training was truly the spiritual equivalent of breaking new ground in a culture where misinformation is rampant and sexual discussion is taboo. Sixty people attended this track and heard American doctors review facts of HIV transmission, symptoms, and prevention. Together, they studied what the Bible has to say about many aspects related to AIDS. Also they heard testimonies of discrimination against those who are HIV positive.

One HIV-positive pastor cast a vast ministry-vision when he "expressed burning determination to give every minute of his life to reaching others for the Kingdom of God," one of our participating doctors reported. "In the face of his example, they caught some of his passion to take the gospel to those dying with AIDS."

"This week's phenomenal success rests squarely on the prayer that surrounded it," that doctor noted. AIMS' network of prayer partners had been fully mobilized. In addition, one hundred intercessors met for nine hours a day during the conference to pray especially for this event. Another twenty-five continued that work on-site. And one hundred intercessors in the U.S. supported this event by prayer and fasting for forty days prior to the event.

All together, our on-site representatives estimated that five to six thousand people were praying for this multi-track event, and many were praying specifically for the AIDS training. A participating missionary doctor told us, "The answers to prayer were very specific. The teaching team, none of whom had met before preparing for this course, found themselves complementing one another's gifts beautifully. Those with little teaching experience received clear anointing to make up any lack."

The results were truly miraculous. At the end of that AIDS training session, participants wrote specific ministry objectives that they wanted to accomplish in their churches and communities. One of the American doctors who led sessions told us, "The total of those plans, if accomplished, could be like fire dropped into dry grass on the vast prairies of Ethiopia."

Prayer Resources

You might not be accustomed to this type of prayer emphasis. You might need some additional information to get started. So let me offer some ideas that anyone can use for cross-cultural intercession.

First of all, whether you are talking about individual or corporate prayer, I suggest that you develop a strategic system. You may want to pray for every nation of the world in the course of a year. Patrick Johnstone's book *Operation World* is an excellent resource for those who wish to pursue this type of intercession. It lists each country and outlines its history and culture, as well as giving specific prayer points.

Alternatively, you may want to adopt a specific country, or even a specific city, for more intensive prayer. At AIMS, we recommend adopting a specific unreached people group—an ethnic or cultural group that needs outside help for evangelization. For instance, you could target your prayers to the country of Mali in West Africa, the city of Bamako in Mali, or the Fula people who live in Mali.

You can do this as an individual, a family, a small group, or an entire congregation. It will give strategic focus to your intercession, as you begin to research and discover specific needs. Additional resources are available on the web.

I encourage you to ask God how he wants you to engage in E1, E2, and E3 praying on behalf of those who have yet to respond to the gospel. Luis Bush, an extraordinary missions mobilizer who founded the AD2000 & Beyond Movement, has recorded hundreds of answers to prayer occurring in the world's hardest-to-reach areas. God is pouring out his Spirit in a miraculous way, and Bush believes this response rests on the focused prayer of millions of believers. He points out that, if the world's 50 million Christians would each intercede for just five minutes per day for thirty days on behalf of those who have never heard the gospel, the net result would be more than fourteen thousand years of prayer.[9]

Bush adds, "We acknowledge the tremendous work that has been done through pioneering missionaries and prayer warriors long before recent prayer movements, partnership, or alliances were formed. The harvest we reap today is the result of the seed they sowed—many times with their blood."[10] Those people recognized the truth of God's Word. They were willing to put in the hard labor of clearing the land.

In God's plan there is always work to be done in the process of clearing out the things that hamper the effective and fruitful sowing of his gospel. Those things include political and religious regimes that are hostile to Christianity. They include the sin that breeds social injustice and poverty. These things will never succumb to human effort, but prayer will uproot them.

Sow This Book into Your Life

Ray Hollowell, a friend who grew up on a farm in North Carolina, remembers his father and brothers clearing thirty acres of new ground. Until the fifth year of labor the land was so rough, Ray's family couldn't use regular farming equipment on it.

Ray explains, "It takes planning, time, and effort to begin to get a profitable harvest from new ground. In northeastern North Carolina, it will take five to ten years of careful husbandry before the new ground will be as productive as the land already in cultivation." He adds, "Before mechanical equipment was available, clearing new ground was a lifetime or multigenerational project."

What does that imply about clearing land for a spiritual harvest? Ray says, "It is not surprising that in some areas of the world, we are just beginning to see significant results from the efforts of missionaries who began the work of clearing the land and cutting down the timbers of false religion fifty, a hundred, and even two hundred years ago. This doesn't mean we can't learn from past mistakes. But we need to be careful about how we criticize their efforts, and cautious about how we evaluate their results."

I agree. We also have to be careful about how we evaluate results of current ministries. We live in a culture that expects instant results. Yet, if Jesus truly intended his people to adopt an agricultural paradigm in relationship to the process of growing his kingdom, we must accept that results require both effort and time.

Since you may not see immediate return for your investment, are you and your church willing to devote resources—money, time, and people—to clearing the land? Explain your answer.

_____

_____

_____

This chapter talks about a specific ministry resource that is available to every individual and every church—prayer. Without clearing the land through intercession, harvest will never happen.

An elder from a church, in Virginia, told us her church has grown by more than 50 percent in the previous five years. She attributed at least 40 percent of that growth to conversions rather than transfer or biological growth. On a scale of one to ten, she ranked her congregation as "ten" in praying for one another, praying for breakthrough in their own community and culture, and praying for spiritual breakthrough in a specific people group(s) of another culture.

She defined the crucial elements for an effective prayer ministry. Given her church's success in mobilizing a powerful intercessory outreach, her answer is enlightening. She told us that an effective prayer ministry:

- Involves private and corporate intercessory prayer
- Targets specific areas for prayer with spiritual warfare to destroy the plots and schemes of the enemy
- Requires church leaders to be present at intercessory prayer, and to teach members how to pray

Given her answers, prayerfully examine your own church and answer these questions:

1. Is intercessory prayer a priority for the pastor and for the leadership team at our church?

_____

If not, why?

_____

_____

_____

2. If it is, does the congregation know it's a priority? How is it modeled?

_____

_____

_____

3. Are your pastor and leadership team praying for the lost in addition to remembering the needs of the congregation?

_____

_____

_____

4. Through what specific venue do you encourage your congregation to be involved in intercession?

_____

_____

_____

5. Is your congregation praying for the lost in addition to remembering the needs represented in your own group?

_____

_____

_____

6. How are you encouraging E1, E2, and E3 praying among your leadership team and your congregation?

_____

_____

_____

In preparation for chapter 7, read:

    Matthew 13:1–23

    Mark 4:1–20

    Luke 8:1–15

chapter 7 < preparing the soil

My friend Albert has harvest mentality so deeply ingrained, he prays for Jesus to delay his return as long as possible. He has no selfish ambition or desire to experience something specific before Jesus calls him home. He simply wants to allow time for more people to come into God's kingdom. Albert told me about an acquaintance who had been released from prison about a year previously. This man started attending Albert's church. Albert challenged him to bring his friends to a service. The young man resisted, saying that he had responded to the gospel after watching Albert for the entire year to determine if his walk matched his talk. He concluded that it did. But he felt unprepared to share the gospel with his friends. Albert said, "You bring them, and *I'll* talk to them."

That young man brought thirty-five friends to church. The pastor explained the gospel. Twenty-five were saved, and twenty became members, giving Albert's church the opportunity to disciple them and help them grow in the faith.

Albert saw a twenty-five-fold harvest in one day, but it was not just one day's worth of work. Those results grew from a year of faithful integrity witnessed by a young man who then responded to Albert's example and agreed to bring his friends to experience the same influence. Albert is devoted to harvest, but he also knows the importance of preparing the soil.

The Parable of the Sower

Matthew 13, Mark 4, and Luke 8 record Jesus' story of a man planting grain. On the Jewish timetable, this would have occurred between October and January when early rains softened the soil for plowing and planting. The plow was usually a simple piece of wood with a metal point attached, fastened by a yoke to one or two oxen or other beasts of burden. The farmer would follow the plow which broke up the soil. He would then spread the seed by hand. Or he might take a sack, punch holes in it, fill it with grain, and lay it on the backs of the oxen, so the seed would fall as the animals moved around.[1] The plowing motion would cover the seed with a light dusting of soil.

In this particular story, Jesus said the seed fell on different kinds of ground.

The Path

Common ground was divided into long narrow strips, and each farmer could cultivate his piece as he wished. The plots were not fenced but were divided by pathways. Anyone could use them for right-of-way, so "they were beaten hard as pavement by the feet of countless passersby."[2] The seed that fell there was exposed, and hungry birds ate it before it had a chance to sprout.

Rocky Soil

This was probably a place where a thin layer of soil covered a vast expanse of limestone. Philip Keller notes, "Seed dropped into such shallow soil will spring up quickly. Rocks retain both heat and moisture. So in this apparently favorable ground the seedlings appear to get off to a quick start. Sad to say, the sudden burst of green is short lived."[3]

Among the Weeds

At the time for sowing, this ground would have looked like a well-prepared plot. Biblical scholar William Barclay explains, "It's easy to make a garden look clean by simply turning over the soil." But if weeds have not been pulled out—if they have matured and gone to seed—those seeds remain in the earth and sprout when conditions are right.[4] Weeds always sprout more quickly and grow more strongly than grain. In the end, they steal space and sunshine that would have made the grain thrive, and they choke the life from the good seed.

Good Soil

Some of this seed landed in a field that was adequately prepared to accept and nurture it. As a result, Jesus said, "it produced a crop—a hundred, sixty or thirty times what was sown" (Matthew 13:8).

Jesus gave the application to His disciples: the seed represents the message of God's kingdom. The path represents those whose hearts are hard so that, when they hear the message, Satan is able to snatch it away. The rocky soil represents those who hear it and receive it, but the roots never grow deep enough to sustain growth. The weedy, thorny soil represents those who hear the message, but their worries choke the life from the developing plant. The good soil represents those who hear the word, understand it, take it to heart, and apply it to their lives. They multiply themselves.

In this harvest parable, the difference between reaping and not reaping is soil preparation. As Phillip Keller reminds us, "It is important to recognize . . . that rocky soils, weed-infested ground, and land lost to pathways were considered non-productive. They were simply incapable of growing a crop in their own natural condition." He adds, "Only the painstaking labor and loving care of a diligent owner could alter their condition. It required tremendous toil . . . to break up the hard ground; to clear stony soil; to cultivate and clean up weed-choked land. . . . *Even the best of soil must first be broken before it can become beautiful.*"[5]

Prayer Is an Effective Plow

Prayer is an effective "plow" for breaking up and softening people's hearts to receive the gospel. It also removes the thorns and weeds that choke out the good news of God's kingdom.

Zephaniah 3:17 hints at this. The King James Version tells us, "The LORD thy God in the midst of thee is mighty; he will save, he will rejoice over thee with joy; he will rest in his love, he will joy over thee with singing." I always thought that was interesting—that God will rest in his own love. But in the Hebrew, the word translated "rest" is *charash*, which means "to scratch, to engrave or to plow."[6] God will plow a place for himself in people's hearts, and it will be a place where he can rest.

When we pray, we can see that promise fulfilled among those we long to see respond to the gospel. We can ask God to plow a place for himself in their hearts. John Nevius, a seasoned Presbyterian missionary with experience in China, understood this principle. Nevius went to Seoul, Korea, in 1890 when Protestant missionaries were seeing limited success. It was still a hard field requiring much plowing and soil preparation. Nevius and others invested years in spiritual warfare, preparing the field for future harvest and birthing a vision that has become a model for indigenous church planting worldwide.

The long-term result is that the Korean church has been described as the "birthplace of revival." Pyongyang, now the capital of North Korea, was 13 percent Christian by 1945, and at least 400,000 Christians lived in the northern part of the country. Many were martyred or fled when communism rose there, but the long-term results of Nevius' work is that the underground church continues to bear fruit. In South Korea, more than one-third of the population is now Christian. The first Protestant church was planted there in 1884, and within one hundred years, South Korea had thirty thousand Protestant churches. In fact, Seoul, Korea, where Nevius landed in 1890, is now almost 40 percent Christian. This city is home to over seven thousand churches, including half of the world's twenty largest churches.[7]

A Contemporary Example

At AIMS, we saw this same principle at work in Burkina Faso in West Africa. Burkina Faso is home to about seventy-seven distinct ethnic groups that come from four major language families. A little over 18 percent of the population is Christian. About 50 percent are Muslim, and about 31 percent practice traditional religions. The remaining portion, less than 1 percent of the population, is non-religious or Baha'i.[8]

In November of 2000, AIMS partnered with some U.S. and Burkinabe churches to sponsor a training conference. Our goal was to mobilize the 18 percent of the population that is Christian and train them to evangelize and plant churches among the thirty-two ethnic groups in Burkina Faso who remain virtually untouched by the gospel. We were amazed that 3,500 pastors and church leaders attended the event.

AIMS staff members who traveled to Burkina Faso to help teach the sessions told us, succinctly, that "plans went awry."

The manuals were not completed according to specifications; the computerized seminar presentations simply didn't work; one speaker lost his voice; and the schedule didn't go as planned. "But, because of prayer," said one staff member, "something marvelous was happening."

We at AIMS, along with our ministry partners, had bathed this event in prayer. The Burkinabe people prayed fervently. Our network of AIMS intercessors was fully mobilized, as were friends and family of participating staff members. In addition, two partner churches took this on as a prayer emphasis. One church fasted for twenty-one days. Another established a twenty-four-hour prayer vigil.

What was the result? Our AIMS staff member reported, "As our plans continuously changed, a sense of God's presence grew. We had no graphs or charts to explain statistics. No graphics to illustrate key missions vocabulary words. But it was no problem! The Lord provided stories and living parables which more deftly fit the African context."

Through that conference, God established on-going partnerships of churches in Burkina Faso and elsewhere. They began the process of uniting their efforts to evangelize and establish churches in Burkina Faso's remaining thirty-two unreached people groups. That kind of long-term result comes from taking the time and making the effort to prepare the spiritual soil to receive the spiritual seed.

Improving and Protecting Soil Fertility

A second aspect of soil preparation involves improving or protecting fertility. Archeologists and biblical scholars tell us that, to protect soil fertility, Hebrew farmers practiced four main strategies:[9]

Fallowing

We discussed this in chapter 3.

Crop Rotation

This means a farmer did not plant the same crop in the same field two years in a row. This way, since different plants require different nutrients, no single element was completely stripped from the land.

Terracing

Farmers improved steep inclines by terracing with stone fences to limit soil erosion. Terracing also helped maintain fertility by accumulating organic matter and minerals to provide a natural method of composting.

Fertilization

This included a limited amount of manure spreading, which could have been accomplished by allowing animals to graze on fallow fields. David C. Hopkins, who has extensively studied agriculture in Israel during the Iron Age, notes a few biblical references implying the use of compost, but he writes that farmers may have reserved this precious resource for vegetable gardens that were close to their homes.[10]

Composting Enriches Soil

Many agriculturalists still see the wisdom of those biblical methods for protecting and even improving soil fertility. Farmers still rotate crops, and some still spread manure. Many backyard gardeners have compost piles to benefit their crops in at least three ways: (1) it attracts living organisms that support healthy agriculture; (2) it helps aerate and loosen the soil; (3) it compensates for drainage problems occurring when the ground has too much clay, thus retaining water, or too much sand, thus allowing water to escape or evaporate.

Compost has tremendous long-term benefit for harvest. Yet this resource is nothing more than decomposed organisms. To improve soil organically, something has to die.

Ruth says her autumns in Pennsylvania were marked by brisk, cool breezes stripping leaves from the maple trees in the backyard. The family spent at least one Saturday afternoon each year raking and heaping them behind the garage. The leaves decomposed over the winter, making rich compost for spring gardening.

In applying composting to our spiritual metaphor of agriculture, God may give you a specific set of applications designed just for you. As I have thought and prayed through this issue, I believe he has revealed general areas where he wants us to allow the wind of his Holy Spirit to strip away some attitudes and habits. As they die and fall to the ground, they will become rich spiritual compost, improving fertility of the soil where God intends for us to sow our seeds. When we allow God to strip away our own negative attitudes and habits, we demonstrate the kind of life that God can use to catch the attention of those in our own culture and in other cultures, preparing them to hear the gospel and respond to it.

Stripping Away Self-Gratification

As we saw in Albert's story, a life of personal integrity prepares spiritual soil to accept the gospel. This supports the opinion of Jim Petersen, who has written classic books on lifestyle evangelism. Petersen describes his early attempts. "Some people became Christians as a result of my efforts," he says, "but the casualty rate was almost as high as the birth rate. I simply explained away my poor results with the parable of the sower: Poor soil—it was their fault, not mine."

Since then, Petersen's success has led him to believe that quick responses come where the soil has already been prepared. Poor results are "the predictable outcome whenever we try to maintain a reaping mentality while evangelizing among unprepared peoples."[11]

Seeing harvest as a process rather than a one-time event, Petersen observes two primary New Testament methods of evangelism: proclamation and affirmation. He defines *affirmation* as "the process of incarnating and demonstrating the Christian message."[12]

Petersen does not negate the necessity of proclamation. He simply notes that affirmation must accompany it. He believes affirmation is particularly "effective among the unprepared—that is, people without a Christian heritage and for whom Christianity does not constitute a credible basis for their lives." Petersen explains, "With rare exceptions, drawing such individuals into the kingdom of God requires more than a summary statement of the gospel."[13] By our lifestyle, we earn the respect that yields a positive response when we proclaim the gospel.

Thus, if we intend to reap a fruitful harvest, we must be willing to prove that whole-hearted submission to Jesus Christ impacts how we live. The apostle Paul clearly tells us that kind of transformation happens only by the renewing of our minds (Romans 12:2), so we can safely assume that, at the most basic level, knowledge and application of Scripture will launch Christ's disciples into new thought and behavior patterns.

Sadly, statistical data reveals a current picture mirroring the portrait painted by the prophet Hosea: "My people are destroyed from lack of knowledge" (Hosea 4:6). Christian researcher George Barna tells us, for instance, that at least in the United States, "the most widely-known Bible verse among adult and teen believers is 'God helps those who help themselves'—which is not actually in the Bible, and actually conflicts with the basic message of Scripture." Barna also notes "less than one out of every ten believers possesses a biblical worldview as the basis for his/her decision-making or behavior." And, he adds, "When Christian adults were asked to identify their most important goal . . . not a single person said it was to be a committed follower of Jesus Christ, or to make disciples of Christ."[14]

That lack of biblical knowledge fuels an attitude that Charles Colson labels "Hot Tub Religion." He writes, "The roots of the church's identity crisis are found in the consumer mentality so pervasive in our culture." The church has become "just another retail outlet and just another commodity," submitting to pressure to increase membership and attendance by adjusting to the "culture of narcissism."[15] That culture supports a general view that God's most basic desire is for his followers to be happy.

Barna sees the results of that view. Survey after survey, he says, reveals that behavior among Christians is no different than their secular counterparts. Perhaps that is most clearly revealed in statistics related to divorce. Barna notes that, in this new spiritual environment in the United States, Christians are actually *more* likely than non-Christians to experience divorce. These raw statistics don't account for people whose divorce occurred before they were converted, nor do they account for people who may have been married to an unbeliever and their partner filed for divorce. But the sad fact remains: the divorce rate among atheists and agnostics is six full percentage points lower than that of people who claim to be born again. Even taking into account certain legitimate explanations for the higher divorce rate among Christians, it is a sad indictment for believers.[16]

Issues like these must be addressed for the sake of misguided Christians whose behavior reflects a basic level of biblical ignorance. For their own benefit in avoiding the entanglements of sin, we must call Western believers back to a commitment to biblical knowledge, understanding, and application. These issues must also be addressed, however, for the sake of the harvest. Self-gratification must be stripped from our lives. As it dies and is placed on the compost heap, it will prepare the soil represented by the lives around us, improving our ability to reap an effective harvest as we sow the seed of the gospel.

Our Superficial Differences Must Die

Patrick Johnstone's *Operation World* lists a series of trends to watch in Europe. Among those items is "ethnic fragmentation." Johnstone notes, "Even as the EU [European Union] expands, the vexed issue of ethnic nationalisms in the UK, France, Spain, Central Europe, Belgium, the Hungarian minorities, and the Russian federation has grown in significance." He briefly discusses the rise of racism in various, well-documented clashes. He concludes, "This is a challenge to Christians to demonstrate Christ's love and that the power of the gospel transcends culture."[17]

Similarly, the United States is increasingly divided. Statisticians reveal very different answers, value systems, and priorities among individuals, based on region, ethnicity, religion, and age.

Unfortunately, these differences also permeate our

churches. Congregations split over musical tastes, worship styles, and sanctuary decorations. One friend jokingly told us she had seen so many church splits, she'd concluded it was her denomination's official church planting strategy. "A few people get mad. They go down the street and plant another church, and then you've got two," she said.

Daily we hear of churches or denominations that refuse to work together because of theological disagreement. Some believers debate sovereignty and free will. Others argue over contemporary applications of the gifts of the Holy Spirit. Still others discuss the timing of Jesus' return to this earth. The list of disputes continues ad nauseam. In the meantime, we lose sight of the necessity of harvest, because we focus on proving our theological correctness.

Am I saying these issues don't matter? No. They matter—but they should not divide us.

It is true; God can use divisions as he did when Paul and Barnabas parted ways, creating two missionary teams instead of one. Furthermore, we must not sacrifice theological purity solely for the sake of harmony. We must maintain the fundamental beliefs that set Christianity apart from other religions.

Truly, however, many of the irrelevant debates that divide the Body of Christ are nothing more than superficial differences. When we resort to petty name-calling and break fellowship with other believers over matters of preference, we reflect the influence of our culture more than the influence of Scripture which tells us, "How good and pleasant it is when brothers live together in unity!" (Psalm 133:1).

Our inability to get along limits our harvest. E. Stanley Jones, long-time missionary to India, told of a large group from southern India, a caste called the Ezhavas who decided to convert to Christianity. Jones described the event, noting,

"After the decision a lawyer arose and said: 'Now you have decided to be Christians. What kind of Christian will you be—Church of England, Baptist, or some other denomination? Now you are united as a caste. In the future you will be divided as these denominations are.'" Jones noted, "They never became Christians. That killed it."[18]

That is a cross-cultural example, but I believe the application is just as true in any type of spiritual harvest. That is why, on the night he was arrested, Jesus spent a lot of time praying for his followers, and his primary request was unity. "My prayer is not for them alone," Jesus said. "I pray also for those who will believe in me through their message, that all of them may be one, Father, just as you are in me and I am in you. May they also be in us *so that the world may believe that you have sent me.*" Later he added, "May they be brought to complete unity *to let the world know that you sent me and have loved them even as you have loved me*" (John 17:20–21, 23, italics added).

I don't subscribe to "unity for unity's sake," but I do subscribe to "unity for evangelism and missions." We must allow the Holy Spirit to strip away superficial differences. They must die and be placed on the compost heap.

Stripping Away Our Individualistic Tendencies

Scripture tells of many people who stood alone against evil. Elijah, for instance, resisted 450 prophets of Baal, challenging them to a spiritual duel. He said, "Put a sacrifice on the altar, but don't light it. See if your god will burn it up." The priests failed. Then Elijah put his sacrifice on the altar. Making it as hard as possible for God to respond, he poured water over the sacrifice, soaking the altar. He even dug a trench to hold the water that ran off. But Scripture tells us, when Elijah prayed, "the fire of the LORD fell and burned up the sacrifice, the wood, the stones and the soil, and also licked up the water in the trench" (1 Kings 18:38). The end result was spiritual harvest, as the Hebrew people experienced a mighty revival in the wake of this contest.

Based on that example, some might say individualism is a good thing. It can help a person stand against peer pressure and against evil. But Elijah's actions were not fueled by a desire to be seen as an individual. They were fueled by the desire to serve and obey God. His identity was anchored in his relationship with God, and his actions were the natural expression of that.

By contrast, George Barna tells us that U.S. believers are having an identity crisis. Based on his surveys, he says they "think of themselves as individuals first, Americans second, and Christians third." He adds, "Until that prioritization is rearranged the Church will continue to lose influence, and biblical principles will represent simply one more option among the numerous worldviews that Americans may choose from."[19]

Scripture gives a very different vision for God's people. It calls us to:

- make his will our priority and his glory our pursuit, seeing our spiritual birth as an initiation into a new identity (1 Peter 2:9–10);

- imitate his example in seeking and initiating relationships with others—saved and unsaved (Romans 5:6–8);

- see ourselves as members of the body of Christ—the church—and use our gifts within that body as a testimony of God's grace (for example, see Romans 12:4–8).

In pursuit of harvest, Christians must submit to these scriptural attitudes. We must create an environment where the commitment to individualism will die. Why?

- Individualism stifles personal accountability which is crucial for preparing spiritual soil among the people God has placed on our hearts, through the daily behavioral expression of our love for Christ.

- It fuels division rather than unity, as people pursue their rights and desire to be seen as individuals with their own opinions and preferences.

- It puts personal agenda ahead of God's plan.

- It causes Christians to avoid building relationships which, in turn, limits opportunities to witness.

In short, the go-it-alone mentality runs counter to God's plan. He wants to demonstrate his love through the ministry of a body of believers, working together in harmony, for the purpose of growing his kingdom. We must allow the wind of the Holy Spirit to strip away our devotion to individualism. As it dies and is placed on the compost heap, it will enhance the soil in the places and among the people where God has called us to sow the seed of the gospel.

The Mystery Garden

Ruth has a mystery garden. She and her husband saved food scraps all winter. Carrot peelings, coffee grounds, and various other trash items went into a special bin for composting. Apparently some seeds were thrown into the mixture—guts from squash, or unconsumed tomatoes or cucumbers that had rotted in the fridge. This spring, when they buried the compost, it began to sprout. Now they have a mystery garden. They don't even know what some of the plants are, but they are eagerly waiting to see the fruit.

Composting is always useful for improving the soil, but often it yields its own harvest. In the spiritual realm, you might not even know you are planting seeds; you might go about your business, naturally revealing Christ's influence on your life through your choices and your behavior. You see the personal growth in your own relationship with God as you live your life according to his desires. And yet, when all is said and done, you will find that you have reaped a harvest in the lives of others, simply because they were watching while you were being faithful to God's call and allowing him to change you from the inside-out.

Sow This Book into Your Life

1. In this chapter, we've covered a lot of territory. Briefly review the three things I believe must be stripped from the lives of Western Christians to fuel a harvest mentality. Discuss their application to your life and to your church.

• Knowing and applying Scripture; how are you doing in this area? And how are your church staff and congregation doing? How do you measure your practices in this area?

_____

_____

_____

_____

• On a scale of 1–10, how unified are your church staff? Your congregation? How willing are you to work with other churches or denominations?

_____

_____

_____

_____

• George Barna's research indicates that American Christians see themselves first as individuals, second as Americans, and third as Christians. How do your personal priorities line up with his list? What about members of your congregation? How do you think they would list themselves? Do you need to address that issue? If so, how?

_____

_____

_____

_____

_____

2. God may have given you more specific applications related to your own situation or your own congregation. He may have brought to mind some other applications—some other things that need to die in order to pursue harvest. List those applications, and discuss them.

_____

_____

_____

_____

_____

3. Churches can do a lot to incarnate the gospel, and thus prepare the soil for greater harvest in their own communities and in other cultures as well. In answering our questionnaire, an associate pastor from Newark, Missouri, told us his church practices a specific brand of "servant ministry"—serving the community through good works, and then demonstrating the reason for their compassionate response. So I invite you to ask yourself:

• What types of servant ministry would be appropriate for your community?

_____

_____

• What types of servant ministry match the spiritual gifts of those in your church?

_____

_____

• Where you find a match in the answers to those two questions, please take some time to determine how you will bring about actual planning and implementation to make that happen in your church and community.

_____

_____

4. This chapter gives two cross-cultural examples of success or failure in soil preparation. Review the example of John Nevius and the situation described by E. Stanley Jones. Based on those examples, describe how the principles of soil preparation—plowing and composting—can be lived out in cross-cultural ministry. Then explain how that affects your church's responsibility to grow God's kingdom globally.

_____

_____

_____

_____

In preparation for chapter 8, read:
    Isaiah 28:23–29

chapter 8 < matching the seed to the soil

J im moved to Maine from Florida, bringing some of the most beautiful orange seedlings he had "ever laid eyes on" in all his forty years of citrus growing. He lovingly prepared the soil. He carefully dug holes and dropped seedlings into them. He planted a whole grove, expecting a bountiful harvest of oranges just like he had seen on an annual basis in Florida. But so far, . . . nothing. They simply didn't thrive in this place.

We usually think of strategy in terms of athletic competition or military effort, perhaps a business venture—something that involves activity and requires people to develop a "battle plan" or "plan of action." We don't usually think of strategy in terms of something as sedate and pastoral as farming. But Jim's story reveals that a successful farmer always has an intelligent strategy or plan. He has to decide what he is going to plant and where he's going to plant it. Agriculturalists tell us a wise farmer makes those decisions based on these types of considerations:

- type of soil (acidity, sand versus clay, etc.)
- slope of land
- climate (amount of sunlight and rainfall, strength of wind, etc.)
- distance to market
- storage and marketing facilities[1]

If Jim had considered those factors, he probably would not have planted citrus trees in New England. Biblical farmers would have used similar criteria, and they would have selected their crops accordingly. They would have matched their seed to the climate, the topography, and the type of soil. They knew what grew best in their environment.

God's Design for Sowing

The prophet Isaiah tells us agricultural planning is no accident. In the midst of a message on impending judgment for the tribe of Ephraim, he tells us, "Listen and pay attention and hear what I say" (Isaiah 28:23). All three of these commands carry the implication not just of hearing but also of giving undivided attention and then obeying.[2]

Today's culture might be surprised, then, to hear him launch into a series of agricultural questions. "When a farmer plows for planting, does he plow continually? Does he keep on breaking up and harrowing the soil? When he has leveled the surface, does he not sow caraway and scatter cumin? Does he not plant wheat in its place, barley in its plot, and spelt in its field? His God instructs him and teaches him the right way" (Isaiah 28:24–26).

Isaiah also notes that each of those crops must be harvested and prepared in different ways (verses 27–28). Then Isaiah concludes, "All this also comes from the LORD Almighty, wonderful in counsel and magnificent in wisdom" (Isaiah 28:29).

Isaiah describes a farmer who knows that plowing and preparing the soil are not ends in themselves. They are means to harvest, but harvest will never be achieved if we plow forever.

The wise farmer also understands that different seeds require different conditions. According to Levitical law, each crop must be planted in its own place. You couldn't plant wheat and barley in the same field, or even grapes and grain together (see Leviticus 19:19).

So, how does the farmer know what to plant where? Isaiah says God "instructs and teaches" him. In Hebrew, the word translated "instructs" means "to chasten, reprove, or correct." In Deuteronomy 8:5, this word is used to describe a man disciplining his son and God disciplining his children. The word translated "teaches" literally means "to flow as water or to shoot as an arrow." By implication, it means "to point out, as if by aiming the finger."[3]

Furthermore, this passage promises that God will point out the "right way." In Hebrew, this legal term means "a verdict, especially a required sentence, or a divine law." But in the broader sense, it comes from a root word that simply means "to govern."[4] So we are back to the principles of stewardship (governing or ruling the land).

This passage gives practical instruction for spiritual harvest. God has an overall plan for all living things. We could compare this to his general plan to grow his kingdom. He is bringing about harvest in every culture. God also has an explicit plan for the farmer to plant specific crops where they have the best opportunity to thrive. We could compare this to God's particular plan for growing his kingdom in specific communities and cultures. Because God is interested in harvest, he really wants to give his people a vision for both the general and the specific plan. He may "point" or "aim" his finger in a specific direction through revelation, or he may point us toward additional research to discover a strategy that will lead to the goal of spiritual harvest.

P   A   R   A

Where Do We Start?

We will find God's general plan in his Word. His design for growing his kingdom underscores everything recorded from Genesis to Revelation. At the risk of sounding like a broken record, we will discover his specific plan as we pray.

God wants every individual believer and every local church to be involved in the harvest of specific fields. These fields will be in our own culture, in similar cultures, and in cultures that are entirely different from our own. In chapter 6, I explained E1, E2, and E3 evangelism as it relates to praying. That same E1, E2, E3 concept applies to every facet of harvest.

As we pray, God will reveal the fields he has assigned to us. He will also disclose the most effective strategy we can use to steward them into spiritual fruitfulness. As a farmer studies his environment to determine the strategy that will yield the best crop, we also need to research the culture where we minister to discover the best way to sow the seed of the gospel. God will show us the detailed application of Scripture fitting that particular field as we pray.

Most Christians agree that good programs grow from God-inspired ministry vision and that Bible study and prayer unlock that vision. A growing number of Christians participate in prayer movements that God is using to rewrite the future for millions of people all over the world. But most Christians don't really *act* on the understanding that prayer is crucial if we wish to accomplish eternal results. I'm not questioning church programs—I'm simply saying they must begin, continue, and end in prayer.

R.A. Torrey told us, "We do not live in a praying age.

We live in an age of hustle and bustle, of man's efforts and man's determination, of man's confidence in his own power to achieve things, an age of human organization, and human machinery, and human push, and human scheming, and human achievement." He went on to outline the church's adoption of that same value system. He wrote, "The church of Christ was never in all its history so fully and so skillfully and so thoroughly and so perfectly organized as it is today." He compared it to a well-built machine, but he said it had no power, because it neglected prayer.[5]

Torrey wrote that in 1924, yet for many of us, the situation hasn't changed much. In harvest terminology, you could say we have invested our resources in big, efficient tractors that are sitting around the farmyard because they are out of fuel. Strategy is important—but it will never replace prayer.

Developing a Good Strategy

A friend named Alan, who works in a travel agency, laughed with me about a woman who visited his office saying she and her husband needed airline tickets to Austria. He arranged the tickets, but within a few days, her husband called, accusing Alan of incompetence. When the proverbial dust settled, they discovered the woman said Austria, but she meant Australia. Two little letters made a big difference in her travel plan.

Regardless of whether we are planning a trip or laying out a garden, our strategy will grow from crucial data. We must know where we are and where we want to go. Once we establish those points, we can map out the most effective plan to get from here to there. Developing a strategy will begin with basic questions.

Where Are We?

What is my church's plan for harvest? Is it adequate? Is it effectively using the gifts of the staff and congregation, not just in ministry to each other but to the surrounding community and to other cultures?

Where Do We Want to Go?

Based on Scripture, what is God's vision for harvest? How can we get involved?

A Good Strategy Will Be Flexible

A good strategy will include goals and objectives, but it won't be set in stone. It will be flexible, adapting to change.

Military historians tell us Henry V overcame great odds to defeat the French in the fifteenth century, because he was able to adapt to changing conditions. In August of 1415, Henry launched a full-scale invasion of France. By the middle of September, the army was weakened by sickness and desertions, and Henry was left with only about nine hundred men-at-arms and five thousand archers. Then, near the end of October, heavy clouds dumped torrential rains on the French landscape.

On October 25, Henry evaluated his grave situation. Rather than submitting, he found a way to take advantage of it. He strategically lured the French into the plowed, open field between the two armies's positions. Hampered by heavy mud, the French soldiers faltered. British archers began shooting horses which pitched their riders to the ground. Those riders were literally stuck in the mud, unable to rise because of their sixty to seventy pounds of armor. Within about an hour, the French lost eleven thousand soldiers, while the English lost only about a hundred. The British won, because they were able to adapt.[6]

You might think flexibility is necessary only in some types of active ventures such as war. But it is required in just about any endeavor. We talked in the previous chapter about crop rotation. A wise farmer doesn't plant the same crop in the same field two years in a row. Different plants require varying minerals and elements, so if you rotate your crops, no single element is stripped from the land. But crop rotation demands flexibility. The farmer must keep track of what he has done, evaluate his success, and alter his plan to protect soil quality and future harvests.

A farmer's flexibility also allows him to try new methods. I heard of an Alabama community that grew cotton annually. For two consecutive years, the dreaded boll weevil devastated the cotton crop in that region, so some farmers started planting peanuts. Those who made the transition eventually paid their debts and grew wealthy. Now that little community has erected a monument in the town square—a monument to the boll weevil, for if that insect had not forced them to alter their agricultural strategy, they would still be struggling to earn a living by planting cotton.[7]

A farming friend told me that story probably dates to sometime between 1900 and 1930. "Many of their children switched back to cotton in the mid-1980s when it once again became profitable to grow cotton. Today, many of those same farmers are looking for new options, since they can no longer compete in the world market growing either crop."

In spiritual harvest, a good strategy will demonstrate that same kind of flexibility—the willingness to adapt to new situations, seeking new, creative methods. A good strategy is a means to an end, not an end in itself. The objective is harvest, and the strategy must adapt to support that goal.

A Good Strategy Will Be Specific
for the Cultural Environment

Albert Mollegen was a respected church leader and theologian from the southeastern, coastal part of Virginia called the Tidewater area. Mollegen once taught a group of lay people on the topic of revelation—the scriptural way that God reveals himself to people. His discussion was full of exegetical analysis and multi-syllabic theological hair splitting. Finally he concluded his lecture and opened the forum for questions. One befuddled woman brought the whole presentation into relevance. "Dr. Mollegen," she asked, "how does God speak to you?"

This well-respected biblical scholar considered her question carefully, then offered a simple, candid answer. "He speaks to me in English," Mollegen quipped, "with a Tidewater accent."[8]

God talks in the vernacular we understand. That is the whole theme of Christ's incarnation—his coming to earth as a man, speaking and living God's plan so we could grasp and imitate it. John 1:14 tells us, "The Word (Jesus) became flesh and made his dwelling among us." Eugene Peterson's paraphrase called *The Message* says, "The Word became flesh and blood, and moved into the neighborhood." God calls us to do that as well—to speak and live the Word so others respond to God's offer of abundant and eternal life. That defines our part in the process of incarnation.

But our method or strategy will change from culture to culture, and even from community to community as we each research our specific situations.

Research Is Necessary,
Even in Your Own Culture

Most people readily admit that research is crucial for cross-cultural ministry. If we have not lived in and are not familiar with the culture where God has called us to minister, we need to prayerfully study the people and their habits and preferences.

This is equally valid in our own community. As Western culture changes, the evangelical church is increasingly becoming a sub-culture—a group that holds to its own set of rules for living, often ignoring the people around them who have a completely different mindset.

Jim Petersen describes an apparent "boom" in evangelical Christianity. He notes, "Anyone can verify this fact by the simple exercise of working his way through the Sunday morning traffic jam surrounding any one of the many super-churches." But he adds, "The euphoria that seems to characterize these churches, as the overworked pastoral staffs attempt to cope with their own success, gives little occasion to pause and reflect on the bigger picture." Petersen notes, "The religious trend we just described, impressive as it may be, is not mainstream. It is a countercurrent that is decidedly distinct from the broad flow of society. In terms of size and impact, the secularized mainstream exerts an overwhelming influence."[9]

Simply put, the secular people who live around us—those who make up our harvest field—don't see life as we do. They don't have the same values. They don't even talk the same language.

Leonard Sweet describes a group of pastors who went to a "March Madness" college basketball championship game.

Seeing the ubiquitous fan with the "John 3:16" sign, the pastors overheard fans debating the sign's meaning. Sweet writes, "Reduced to guessing, one thought it must be an ad for a new restaurant in town. The others dissed [disrespected] that idea since 'who would send someone out with orange hair and a hand-drawn sign to advertise anything?' Another thought the 'John 3:16' sign might be a signal to someone to meet at the John on the third floor, stall 16." Sweet concludes, "Talk about clueless. They were totally in the dark why anyone would be holding a sign with those words on it."[10]

We Christians can no longer rely on our society to understand *christianese*. Nor can we trust our own counterculture knowledge to plan a successful evangelistic strategy. We must research the community we want to reach, whether it is on the other side of the world, or just down the street.

We do not have space to give an exhaustive list of suggestions for this type of research. Demographic information is a good place to start. That will include broad information like age breakdowns, average income, ethnicities, and other similar statistics that often are available from the local chamber of commerce or from the census bureau. The local newspaper often takes census information and explains how it applies to or reflects your community. George Barna's research group provides statistical information on a host of topics related to communities in the United States. We have extensively cited this organization in our notes and bibliography, so please refer to those lists for additional information. We also have cited several resources that address ministry in contemporary Western culture. For ministry to specific neighborhoods, consider formulating your own survey and using it to collect information. For additional suggestions, especially as they relate to researching unfamiliar cultures, please see the appendix at the back of the book.

This kind of research will lay a foundation for a specific strategy for the cultural and spiritual environment where you minister. It also might be wise to research and discover your own strengths and weaknesses. This is important for individual Christians hoping to improve personal harvesting skills, or for church leaders hoping to breathe new life into a sagging evangelism and missions program. Prayerfully analyze the spiritual gifts and resources God has put within you or within your congregations. Examine the nature of the community and culture he has assigned to you. Then, based on Bible study, prayer, and research, ask God for his specific strategy.

A Good Strategy Doesn't Copy Someone Else's Success

Western technocrats love "how to" manuals with "one-two-three" explanations. We are comfortable with mathematical formulas, plugging numbers into variables to gain easy answers. The Bible is God's "how-to manual," yet it clearly demonstrates that God's will and way can never be reduced to a formula.

The prophet Isaiah outlined this paradox when he wrote, "Forget the former things" (Isaiah 43:18), and then cautioned, "Remember the former things" (Isaiah 46:9). Remember God's deeds, for they build your faith. But resist the temptation to turn history into a pre-fabricated blueprint for success. In the same way, while we learn from those who have successful strategies, we shouldn't import them wholesale into our own fields. That negates the principle that God has a precise strategy for every situation.

Using a specific example, Leonard Sweet explained, "It's amazing to me that people look at a church like Willow Creek . . . and say, 'We should be like that.' Willow Creek is a unique church. There is only one Willow Creek. To seek simple formulas for complex missions is to incubate mediocrity if not misconduct of mission. One person's plan is another person's poison."[11]

So learn to be comfortable in the paradox. Remember the "former things," but at the same time, forget them, and ask God to do a new thing.

Sow This Book into Your Life

The senior pastor of a church in Wilmington, Delaware, mentioned on a questionnaire that his church is only about eight-years-old, but almost half of its membership can be attributed to conversions rather than transfer or biological growth. As part of their evangelistic strategy, this church built a skate park where they reach out to young people who use it.

That strategy works in Wilmington, but it wouldn't necessarily transfer well to a church in Newark, Missouri, which an associate pastor described as a rural community where many people are older. They probably wouldn't be interested in a skate park.

A successful strategy can't necessarily be transplanted. God has a specific design for you and your church. As you seek his will and develop a plan of action, ask yourself these questions:

1. Where are the fields that God has assigned to my church and me? Consider those in your own culture, in similar cultures, and in completely different cultures. You may need to do some research to determine cross-cultural fields, and frankly, this may require some additional time. But go ahead and start the process here.

_____

_____

_____

2. What do you know about the spiritual and cultural environment in those fields? How can you learn more?

_____

_____

_____

3. God has already invested great resources and spiritual gifts within you and your congregation for the purpose of harvest. What are they?

_____

_____

_____

4. Based on Bible study, prayer, and the information you gain through research, what specific plan does God have for you to steward your assigned fields into fruitfulness?

_____

_____

_____

In preparation for chapter 9, read:

Mark 4:1–20, 26–29

Ecclesiastes 11:4–6

P A R A

chapter 9 < sowing the seed

I n the 1920s, a Russian scientist named Nikolai Vavilov assembled a legion of 26,000 assistants who traveled the globe, collecting seeds and bringing them to the world's first major seed bank in Leningrad. Over twenty years, Vavilov and his aides transported, labeled, and stored seeds from about 200,000 species. Then, because of a difference of scientific opinion with a Stalinist competitor, Vavilov was imprisoned and finally died in 1943.

Russia was engaged in World War II. The Nazi war machine attacked in June 1941. The terrible siege of Leningrad-St. Petersburg lasted about 900 days (September 8, 1941, through January 27, 1944). At least 600,000 people starved to death.

Still, Vavilov's botanists continued his work. When they ran out of food, they chose to starve rather than endanger the collection by eating the seeds. Some may debate the wisdom of their decision, but no one could doubt their commitment to an ideal, anchored in their understanding of the seed's true value. These men truly believed the seed's future worth outweighed its current value as a quick meal.[1]

The Value of a Seed Lies in What It Does on Its Own

Seeds carry the secret of life. In the right surroundings, they sprout and grow all on their own; that is the essence of their value. Man has very little to do with their ability to grow, except as we alter their environment. We can improve the soil. We can ensure the optimal amount of water. To a certain degree, we can control the amount of light and heat they receive. But the seed itself sprouts, grows, and reproduces itself, because that is how God designed it (see Genesis 1:11–12).

Jesus illustrated this fundamental process when he described a man scattering seed. "Night and day," Jesus said, "whether he sleeps or gets up, the seed sprouts and grows, though he does not know how. All by itself the soil produces grain—first the stalk, then the head, then the full kernel in the head. As soon as the grain is ripe, he puts the sickle to it, because the harvest has come" (Mark 4:26–29).

That story follows soon after the "Parable of the Sower," discussed in chapter seven of this book. In explaining that narrative, Jesus said the seed represents God's Word. Given the proximity of the two tales, we can assume the same symbolism here. Jesus used the term *logos*, one of the Greek expressions translated "word." *Logos* denotes "a verbal expression or communication revealing a thought or an idea." In some passages, it refers to the totality of God's messages to man (see Mark 7:13; John 10:35). It also describes Christ himself as the incarnate expression of God (see John 1).[2]

So we see that God's Word—the expression of his character and ideal—makes up the seed that his followers are called to plant into the lives of other people. That Word is like seed in at least two ways: it is alive in and of itself (Hebrews 4:12), and it will not be "planted" without effect (Isaiah 55:11).

The central point of God's Word is the gospel. It is the good news that, because God loves people, he initiates reconciliation for a relationship broken by man's sin. It describes the incarnation of God's Son—fully God and fully man—who lived a sinless life and died a sacrificial death to bridge the gap between God and man. It also expresses Christ's ultimate resurrection that sealed spiritual victory for every individual who would accept Jesus' intervention.

Tradition tells us the British poet Alfred Lord Tennyson was strolling one day when he met General William Booth, founder of the Salvation Army. Tennyson waved and yelled a greeting. "What is the news this morning?" he asked. Booth replied, "The news is that Christ died for our sins and rose for our justification." Tennyson answered, "Ah, that is old news, and new news and good news."[3]

That is the message that Jesus wants his followers to plant into the people around them. The message never changes. Jesus' parable assures us that it will sprout and grow. But to some degree, we contribute to the plant's ability to be well-rooted, to thrive, and to reproduce.

We have already talked about soil preparation and strategy, describing their impact on agricultural success. In essence, while the seed of the message remains constant, everything else must either alter the environment (as in composting) or adapt to it (as in strategizing). In God's plan, ultimate yield is gained primarily through man's involvement and care. God uses his people to sow spiritual seed. We can do all the praying and living and strategizing we want to—I would never diminish the importance of those activities—but if we never actually plant the seed, there will be no harvest.

Sowing Requires Faith

Wise King Solomon warned, "Whoever watches the wind will not plant; whoever looks at the clouds will not reap" (Ecclesiastes 11:4). Conditions are rarely perfect. The farmer knows and accepts that, but he sows anyway, believing the seed will do what God intended and promised. It will grow.

The great nineteenth century preacher Charles Spurgeon made this application: "If a man had not great faith in God, he would not take the little wheat he has, and go and bury it. His good wife might say to him, 'John, we shall want that corn for the children, so don't you go and throw it out where the birds may eat it, or the worms destroy it.'" He compared this to the act of sowing spiritual seed. He said, "You must preach the gospel, and you must teach the gospel as an act of faith. You must believe that God will bless it. . . . If it is done merely as a natural act, or a hopeful act, that will not be enough; it must be done as an act of confidence in the living God."[4]

So, where does that faith come from?

- Studying Scripture and seeing God's promises come to life in our own experiences.

- Meeting God in prayer and leaving that encounter with the full confidence that he will do what he says.

- Accepting faith as God's precious gift, which undergirds and strengthens our obedience.

- Participating in the harvest process and seeing God's faithfulness in bringing fruit from our meager attempts.

Scripture tells us that "faith is being sure of what we hope for and certain of what we do not see" (Hebrews 11:1). The truth of this statement is clearly seen when a farmer plants seeds. There is no visible crop, just a kernel. Even that is not visible once he buries it. Just as the farmer knows his work will bear fruit, we also can trust that our sowing will not be in vain.

Sowing Is Intentional

No farmer would do the hard work of planting crops just for the physical exercise of wandering around his field. He has a purpose. His actions reinforce Henry David Thoreau's opinion, "Though I do not believe that a plant will spring up where no seed has been, I have great faith in a seed. Convince me that you have a seed there, and I am prepared to expect wonders." [5]

No matter what a farmer is doing, harvest is on his mind. Similarly, anyone engaged in spiritual harvest must work intentionally. No matter what we are doing, harvest must be at the forefront of our thinking. For the local church, this means training the staff and congregation to examine every relationship and every conversation for opportunities to connect people with God's Word. We do that by our lifestyle choices, for Jesus told his followers to live so that men would "see your good deeds and praise your Father in heaven" (Matthew 5:16). We also do it by our conversation, for Jesus also told his disciples to "preach the good news to all creation" (Mark 16:15).

Every Christian has daily opportunities to share the gospel—but most of us do not take advantage of them. We are not even aware of them and are not looking for opportunities, so we miss the chance to plant God's perfect Word into imperfect lives. A person who expects God to reveal those opportunities will see them—just like a man named Rigby whose business responsibilities required him to travel regularly throughout Scotland.

Alexander Whyte of St. George's Church in Edinburgh recorded that, when Rigby was in town, he habitually attended St. George's on Sunday, but he never came alone. He always brought someone even if it meant inviting a stranger. This went on for several years before Whyte actually met Rigby.

"Man," Whyte said, "I've been looking for you for years." You see, Whyte received a bundle of notes from people who had attended church with Rigby. Those church visits changed their lives.[6] And it all happened because one businessman watched for those occasions. He regularly and intentionally sowed God's Word into the people he met.

Sowing Is Strategic

As we discussed in the previous chapter, successful planting is based on a plan. That plan has only one goal—to maximize harvest. That strategy, as I explained, must never confuse the seed to be planted with the fruit to be harvested. That is, the gospel seed must remain the same, whatever the strategy for planting and harvesting.

Leonard Sweet describes this principle using a different analogy comparing the gospel to water, which can be stored in all kinds of different containers. He writes, "The mystery of the gospel is this: it is always the same (content) and it is always different (containers)." He notes, "I am a virtual fundamentalist about content. I am a virtual libertarian about containers. Only in Jesus Christ did container and content become one." Citing Jesus' comments about new wine in old wineskins, Sweet reminds us, "We cannot make an idolatry of any form or container. We must not elevate an ecclesial form to the level of authority or primacy that belongs only to the content."[7]

Strategies can be as varied as the situations for which they are developed and as creative as the circumstances require. Still, I've discovered some agricultural principles that seem to increase yield despite the varying conditions in different regions. They apply to spiritual harvest as well.

Variety Is the Sustenance of Life

Champions of natural agriculture, along with a host of botanists and other scientists, have argued for years against the monocultural planting done by many Western farmers. They cite food crises such as the Irish potato famine of 1845–1850, which occurred because a fungus attacked the lumper, the most widely grown potato in Ireland at that time. In 1845, as one writer explained, "The blight rotted its way across the uniform potato population, destroying half the crop. The next year it wiped out virtually the entire crop, . . . and a million people who relied on it died, while another million and a half fled the stricken country."[8]

Many believe the blight would not have wiped out the entire crop if Irish farmers had not relied so heavily on one type of potato. Wendell Berry, who visited Peru to witness efforts of Andean subsistence farmers, noted that the primary crop there is also potatoes. Berry wrote, "The Andean farmers' first principle is variety. It is the ancient wisdom of putting the eggs into several baskets; in a season or a field in which one variety perishes, another, and several others may thrive." Berry recalled one farmer who planted forty-six different kinds of potatoes in a field the size of an average Western living room. Variety will safeguard the harvest, for if one type of potato succumbs to a disease or a fungus, others will resist and thrive.[9]

This principle is not just true for potatoes. I read recently about a stunning new result from one of the largest agricultural experiments ever. Thousands of rice farmers in China "doubled the yield of their most valuable crop and nearly eliminated its most devastating disease—without using chemical treatments or spending an extra penny." Based on research from an international group of scientists, these farmers made one simple change. "Instead of planting the large stands of a single type of rice, as they typically have done, the farmers planted a mixture of two different rices." And what was the result? "With this one change, growers were able to radically restrict the incidence of rice blast—the most important disease of this most important staple in the world. Within just two years, farmers were able to abandon . . . chemical fungicides."[10]

Partnering to Multiply the Harvest

Evangelism and missions work best when they are group efforts. Scripture clearly tells us that God made individuals to be unique. He gave specific talents and abilities to each of us. Then he also gave supernatural gifts. Those characteristics reflect God's creativity—and the differences can be seen as different ways of sowing seed. The message is identical, but the expression is diverse. We need other people to labor with us so that, as a group, we sow seeds in a variety of ways; more effectively mirroring God's character to the world.

Church leaders must understand the abilities inherent in their congregation. Scripture tells us that Christ's followers are to be involved in personal witnessing and testifying to what God has accomplished in their lives. Research indicates that only about 10 percent of the people in every church body are specifically gifted for evangelism. One church growth analyst notes that, unless we mobilize those people, "the 10 percent with the gift of evangelism would be significantly under-challenged, while the demands on the 90 percent without the gift would be too great."[11]

Obviously, engaging that 10 percent is crucial for evangelistic success—in our own culture and in cross-cultural missions as well. But, in our discussion of the "gift of evangelism," we must remember that each of us as Christians is commanded to testify and be a witness about our relationship with Jesus.

Those who have a special gift for evangelism will increase their yield as they partner with others with different gifts. When Jesus called his disciples to be "fishers of men," he was talking to people who made their living fishing. They were not weekend anglers with fly rods; they were men who strained together to pull in large nets of fish for market. If fishing is your hobby, you can do it alone. But if it is your business, you need people to help you.

Every gift that God gives—from administration to hospitality, from teaching to helps and service—has a function in evangelism and missions. The secret is to find the application without demanding some sort of numerical accounting for decisions, which increases the stress and decreases the enjoyment for those not specifically gifted to bring people to the point of making Christ their Savior and Lord.

Teamwork ensures greater harvest, but it also multiplies the power available to achieve the goal. Wise King Solomon wrote, "Two are better one, because they have a good return for their work: If one falls down, his friend can help him up. . . . Though one may be overpowered, two can defend themselves. A cord of three strands is not quickly broken" (Ecclesiastes 4:9–10, 12).

Partnerships at Work

At AIMS, we build alliances of churches, agencies, and individuals who are interested in taking the gospel to a specific region or people group. We consistently see, as ministries work together, they accomplish much more than the sum of what they could accomplish by working separately.

Suppose your church has a vision for ministering in India. You could do it alone—and you would see limited results. But suppose you contact AIMS, and we network you with several other groups who also want to penetrate India with the gospel. One agency specializes in digging wells. Another provides the *Jesus Film* translated into the language of the people you are targeting. A church agrees to provide equipment needed to show the film. Another pays for Bibles for follow-up. If it is an illiterate culture, perhaps an agency can provide the Bible on cassette tape with solar powered or hand-cranked players. Still another agrees to plant churches.

Together you decide that the first agency will dig wells, which will become the gathering place for that particular culture. A missionary—perhaps an Indian Christian who has a call to evangelize in his own country—shows the film, and several Hindu people convert and are baptized. That missionary gives them the Bibles or cassettes and explains what they are reading or hearing. Soon you have planted a church, and by working together, you have produced something much bigger and more effective than what all of you could do by working separately. Almost invariably, partnership—which reflects the diversity suggested by agriculturalists—increases the yield of spiritual harvest.

More Isn't Always Better

In the movie *Sabrina,* a classic line is spoken in which the main character, played by Julia Ormond, looks at Linus Larrabee, a billionaire tycoon played by Harrison Ford, and says, "More isn't always better, Linus. Sometimes it's just more."

Many agriculturalists would agree. Jim Jeavons, for example, grows his crops in raised beds about one hundred square feet in size (about ten feet by ten feet). He claims this enables him to build up soil about sixty times faster than would happen naturally. Those beds require about eight hours of preparation time, and he can maintain them in about fifteen minutes per day. His yield per square foot is at least twice that of the American agricultural average—and with some crops, under certain conditions, it rises to thirty times the productivity of commercial agricultural systems. In addition, Jeavons uses up to 80 percent less water and buys 50 percent less organic fertilizer. Thus he expends 99 percent less energy per pound of food produced.[12]

The spiritual application was expressed in an e-mail our office received from an on-site Ethiopian ministry partner. "Let me tell you," he said, "the expansion of the kingdom of God is not only measured by the quantity of people, but by the quality of the lives of the believers. . . . The church history has proved that mere numerical expansion of churches has ended up in devastation."

His sentiments are echoed in Christian A. Schwarz's book *Natural Church Development.* On the surface, it may look like big churches are more strategic in their planning than small churches. But based on a lengthy study of thousands of churches worldwide, Schwarz noted that smaller churches averaged 13 percent growth, while larger churches averaged only 3 percent growth.

Schwarz summarized, "While the smallest churches (with an average attendance of 51) typically won 32 new people in the last five years, the megachurches (with an average attendance of 2,856) won 112 new persons during the same time period. In raw numbers, a single megachurch won many more people than a single 'minichurch.' . . . If we remember, though, that the megachurches are 56 times the size of the 'minichurches,' then the following calculation expresses the potential of the two categories far more realistically."

Schwarz explains that, if a single mega-church with an attendance of 2,856 people would divide into fifty-six congregations, each with fifty-one worshipers, they would multiply their combined yield sixteen times. Or, as Schwarz writes, "We can conclude that the evangelistic effectiveness of mini-churches is statistically 1,600 times greater than that of megachurches!"[13]

God may give you a specific application for your situation, but on the surface, this leads me to a general conclusion. We must not gauge success merely by size. Schwarz notes that, among the groups he surveyed, only 31 percent of growing churches had established numerical goals for growth. Rather, their goals were qualitative—something like "by the end of November, 80 percent of all regular worship attenders will know their spiritual gifts." The leadership set a different agenda. Numerical growth was no longer the goal—but it *was* the by-product.[14]

Understanding that clarification, we can accept the fact that small churches are strategic. Schwarz noted, "On nearly all relevant quality factors, larger churches compare disfavorably with smaller ones."[15]

With that in mind, I offer two suggestions: (1) We should develop a small-group format linked specifically to evangelism and missions. Schwarz considers "holistic small groups" to be the most important of eight factors that mark a truly healthy church. (2) Rather than growing bigger and bigger churches, we should plant new churches to assimilate continued growth.

Soak Your Seeds

Backyard gardeners know that seeds sprout more quickly if they are soaked in water before they are placed in the soil. At the risk of sounding like this is a book on prayer instead of harvest, (as if the two could be separated) I suggest soaking the seed through intercession.

Dwight L. Moody recognized the value of prayer in planting God's Word. Moody helped provide humanitarian aid in Chicago after the great fire. Then he went to England to rest. He was not intending to preach. Rather he wanted to listen to some of the greatest preachers of that day—Spurgeon, Mueller, and others. But Moody was invited to speak one Sunday in the northern part of London. He preached that morning with great difficulty. He told R.A. Torrey, "I had no power, no liberty; it seemed like pulling a train up a steep grade, and as I preached I said to myself, 'What a fool I was to consent.' As I drew to the close of my sermon I had a sense of relief that I was so near through." Then he remembered—he had to preach again that evening.

Moody related, "I went to the evening service with a heavy heart. But I had not been preaching long when it seemed as if the powers of an unseen world had fallen upon my audience." In the end, he asked all who wanted to receive Christ to stand—and about 500 people rose to their feet. "I thought there must be some mistake," Moody said. "So I asked them to sit down, and then I said, 'There will be an after-meeting in the vestry, and if any of you will really accept Christ, meet the pastor and me in the vestry.'"

The people poured into the vestry. Moody, still not fully believing the results, told them he intended to leave for Ireland, but the pastor would meet with them the following evening. When he arrived in Ireland, Moody received a telegram from the pastor. "There were more people here Monday night than on Sunday night," it said. "A revival has broken out here in our church, and you must come back and help me."

That event launched Moody into international ministry. But what made the drastic difference between the morning service and the evening service? Moody told Torrey of a pair of sisters who were church members. One was bedridden. The other returned from Sunday morning service and said, "You'll never guess who preached this morning. Mr. Moody of Chicago."

The bedridden sister turned pale. "I have read of him in an American paper," she said, "and I have been praying God to send him to London, and to send him to our church. If I had known he was to preach . . . I would have eaten no breakfast, I would have spent the whole morning in fasting and prayer." She quickly remedied the situation, telling her sister to lock the door and refuse to let anyone bother her as she intended to spend the afternoon and evening praying for that evening service. Moody said that was the difference.[16]

Noting that missions and evangelism constitute a declaration of war against Satan, Torrey later concluded, "It is true that we have a terrific fight on our hands . . . but we can win this fight by prayer; for prayer brings God on the field and the devil is no match for him. . . . Men are constantly appearing who have discovered some new way of defeating the devil by some cunning scheme that they have devised. . . . But there is no new way that will win; the old way, the Bible way, the way of definite, determined and persistent prayer in the Holy Spirit, will win every time."[17]

So bathe your seed in prayer—it will exponentially increase your harvest.

Sow This Book into Your Life

1. A senior pastor in Richmond, Virginia, says his church has been learning to live as a true, loving community. Now they are "taking that to the streets." His church emphasizes the "oikos factor." *Oikos* is Greek for "household." It included the immediate family, but also the servants and their families. In contemporary language, your *oikos*, includes the people

within your personal sphere of influence—your family, friends, neighbors, business associates, and others. The New Testament strategy for evangelism relied on individual Christians influencing their *oikos*. If you are an individual, take time to brainstorm. List the people in your *oikos*, and choose three that you think are ready to have seed sown into their lives. Then ask God's direction as you write a strategy outlining how you will do that and how you can partner with others in the process, so you reflect a clearer image of God's character.

If you are a church leader, brainstorm about how you can challenge your church to do that. Remember, modeling is one of the best ways to teach this concept.

_____

_____

_____

_____

_____

_____

2. Several pastors who returned questionnaires noted their current use of, or their desire to move to, a cell- or small-group structure. Yet most saw this primarily as a means to enable their people to minister to one another. Only one or two mentioned small groups in a strategy for evangelism. One of those was a pastor in Richmond, Virginia. At the time that he responded, the church had grown between 10 and 20 percent in the previous five years. He estimated that more than 80 percent of that growth had been through conversions rather than through biological or transfer growth and added, "Our eyes are looking beyond our immediate body—we are aggressively planning for greater future outreach. We avoid proselytizing

other Christians." Describe how small groups in your church could be used for effective seed-sowing.

_____

_____

_____

_____

_____

3. Another pastor from an outreach in Virginia Beach, Virginia told us he gauges his success in evangelism "by the growth and maturity of each person God blesses us to serve." In other words, he measures by "quality rather than numbers." This outreach started with eight people. Within three years there were between 120 and 150, and at least half of that growth was attributed to conversions rather than transfer or biological growth. Describe how this experience fits with the information in this chapter. Compare that to your own experience. How does your church gauge its success? Is this a valid scale for measurement? Why or why not?

_____

_____

_____

_____

4. Many pastors responding to my questionnaire noted particular success either in local evangelism or in cross-cultural missions. Few noted success in both. Yet I believe both are crucial to a church's long-term health and harvest. Without sowing in both fields, we will never achieve God's design laid out in Genesis 1:28 (discussed in chapter 1). We will not

expand to new fields, and eventually we may actually become sterile.

How can your church be involved in planting the seed of the gospel simultaneously in your own church body, in your surrounding community, and in totally different cultures?

_____

_____

_____

_____

In preparation for chapter 10, read:

    Ephesians 4:14–15

    John 8:31–32, 14:6, 17:17

    1 Corinthians 13

    Matthew 13:24–30

    Galatians 5:9

P   A   R   A

chapter 10 < nurturing the crop

"When my children were little," author Mona Riley explains, "we planted carrots and radishes, green beans and tomatoes. All three kids loved to plant the seeds and were thrilled when the shoots emerged. But between the excitement of a strong beginning and the fulfillment of a good crop lay weeks and even months of consistent care. Tiring days spent tending the plants in the sun seemed fruitless when a small, impatient hand pulled up an immature radish and a little voice moaned, 'When will they be ready?'"[1]

Most of us succumb to that same childish expectation. In our fast-paced culture, we demand immediate output for our input. But a harvest mentality means you are in ministry for the long haul. It means you are willing to nurture the crop.

Inadequate Soil Preparation Shows Up Here

Nurturing is a two-fold process. You give the plants what they need to thrive (water and perhaps fertilizer), and you remove or guard against the things that impede or destroy (weeds and insects). If you have effectively prepared the soil, you will greatly minimize your labor of nurturing. As we discussed in chapter 7 of this book, composting aids in moisture retention, reducing the need for watering. It also loosens the soil, so weeds are pulled out easily. Some farmers even claim healthy soil protects against pests over which you have very little control.

Gabriel Howearth is a master organic gardener with fields located in the Rio Grande Valley. As one author explains, Gabriel "observed the simple truth that the health of the soil is the basis of good growing and that disease often represents imbalances or deficiencies in the soil." In an interview, Gabriel "drew a parallel with the body's immune system. He was convinced that good soil management practices virtually eliminate the need for poisonous chemicals."

The author adds that the summer he interviewed Gabriel, a "biblical plague of grasshoppers" had consumed many farms and damaged others. Despite Gabriel's refusal to use pesticides, his garden was the exception; it was not badly hurt. He adds, "Other farmers came to investigate and were impressed by the results of natural farming methods."[2] This farmer used beneficial insects to do away with pests. He also planted certain flowers to attract pests away from his crops. The heart of his strategy, however, rested on the fact that healthy soil yields healthy plants that will resist disease and will not attract pests that consume weak and unstable vegetation.

So soil preparation is not important just for sprouting a crop—it affects the entire process.

The Goal of Nurturing Is to Develop Disciples

Even if you have done a thorough job of soil preparation, you still have some work in the time between sprouting and harvest. You do what you can to help your crop grow to maturity and reach its greatest level of fruitfulness. In the spiritual realm, this defines *discipleship*. The goal is to grow mature believers, and harvest occurs when they are at their peak and can reproduce themselves.

Harvest is more than just evangelism. After all, Matthew

28:18–20 records the Great Commission statement wherein Jesus calls his followers to make disciples—not converts. Our translation "disciple" comes from the Greek word *mathetes*, which means "learner." It implies that a person with that label is "one who professes to have learned certain principles from another and maintains them on that other's authority."[3]

Disciple-making must be the priority of harvest, because it is Jesus' priority. If you are engaged in a ministry that specializes in evangelism, consider partnering with a ministry that specializes in church planting and/or discipleship ministry. At AIMS, we saw this happen in the Former Soviet Union.

When the Iron Curtain crumbled, the Christian Broadcasting Network (CBN) sponsored televised evangelistic broadcasts into the region. The mail response was overwhelming. Since CBN recognized the necessity of nurturing these new converts, they partnered with AIMS to develop strategies to plant churches to assimilate and mentor these new believers. We also partnered with CBN and Regent University to establish a one-year leadership-training center.

Through this joint effort, where several ministries partnered to raise up and train national pastors in Russia and the other fledgling republics, over 3,000 churches have been planted. That immense harvest was based on the principles outlined in this book. We modeled and taught that true discipleship is more than personal discipline. It also includes reproduction. Through this ministry partnership, we have seen young disciples solidified in their faith, pastors mentored in principles of reproduction, new believers come into the fellowships on a regular basis, and then the process begins all over again. But it would have been extremely difficult for any of the participating ministries to accomplish these kinds of results by working alone.

P   A   R   A

How Do You Grow Disciples?

According to one theologian, disciple-making is a three-step process. It includes "introducing people to Christ, building them up in the faith, and sending them into the harvest field." He summarizes this process by what he calls the "three Ds of disciple making: deliver them, develop them, and deploy them."[4]

That fits the harvest paradigm. The process of nurturing parallels the second principle in that list: "develop them." As I've already noted, nurturing a crop involves two distinct activities. We provide the things required for the crop to thrive, and we remove the things that impede, interrupt, or consume growth.

In spiritual harvest, this implies the balance of love and truth, as spelled out in Ephesians, which describes a mature body of believers and explains, "Then we will no longer be infants, tossed back and forth by the waves, and blown here and there by every wind of teaching and by the cunning and craftiness of men in their deceitful scheming. Instead, *speaking the truth in love*, we will in all things grow up into him who is the Head, that is, Christ" (Ephesians 4:14–15, italics mine).

In Western Christianity, many churches emphasize love to the detriment of truth. They accept every kind of person, but in the process they also accept every kind of behavior and doctrine, ignoring biblical standards for purity and righteousness. Charles Colson says these churches "confuse love and permissiveness." He adds, "It is not love to fail to dissuade another believer from sin any more than it is love to fail to take a drink away from an alcoholic or matches from a baby."[5]

Many other churches emphasize pure theology at the expense of love. Mona Riley calls these churches judgmental, noting that they "err on the side of truth without compassion."

She adds that this kind of congregation "probably constitutes the largest group of theologically conservative Christian churches. Though standing for truth, judgmental churches give the law so forcefully that their members forget to mix in Christlike love that exhibits itself in compassion, patience, and willingness to help personally those who deeply desire transformation."[6]

Riley's book primarily discusses homosexuality, but I think her comments ring true to anyone trying to escape sin's bondage. Judgment without compassion does not grow disciples. Nor does compassion without truth. Rather, God's Word calls his people to uphold Scripture's standards—but to do it with an attitude of acceptance born from a respect for the dignity of every individual. That is the essence of speaking the *truth* in *love*. In reality, you cannot have one without the other.

Speaking the Truth

In the original text from Ephesians, the word we have translated "speaking the truth" is *aletheuo*. It is the verb form of the adjective *alethes*, which primarily refers to something that is not hidden. It can describe something factual and true. It also can refer to something that conforms to reality.[7]

A simple statement of belief in the existence of ultimate truth and reality will draw fire from Western culture's politically correct crowd. Yet Jesus plainly preached this, and he even defined it for us. Just before he was betrayed, Jesus prayed for his followers, seeking God's blessing and sustaining power for them in the coming period of agony. Among his requests, Jesus asked God to "Sanctify them by the truth." Then he said, "Your word is truth" (John 17:17).

I believe in the veracity of Scripture. I believe it is the

inspired Word of God—all of it. In keeping with the Greek definition, I believe the Bible is true because it conforms to and describes ultimate reality found only in the character of God. Jesus, as a member of the Trinity, claimed to be *the* Truth (ultimate reality—see John 14:6), and Scripture is true because it conforms to and reflects his ideal.

Speaking the truth, then, requires intimate knowledge and faithful interpretation of Scripture. It requires preaching and teaching of the whole gospel, the good news that undergirds the whole Bible from Genesis to Revelation.

Truth does not always bring immediate comfort. In the agricultural paradigm, it is kind of like weeding—removing things that compete for sunlight and growing space. Subscribing to truth shapes what we say, but it also shapes who we are and how we live. "We like to use words that minimize damage to our self-image, even when we know it's wrong," explains one ministry director. He adds, "We say, 'I got a divorce.' What we really mean is, 'I abandoned my wife.' It's so much more comfortable for us to wrap the truth up in a cleaner package."[8]

Not every divorce can be described as abandonment. Still, the overarching reality of the preceding statement remains. Rather than obeying the truth, most of us will seek a cleaner package even if the wrapping is actually a lie.

If we accept Scripture as truth, we cannot edit out the parts we do not want to obey. It is all good news—even the parts that seem to limit self-expression and personal freedom. After all, Jesus promised, "If you hold to my teaching, you are really my disciples. Then you will know the truth, and the truth will set you free" (John 8:31–32). Truth doesn't limit freedom—it gives birth to it.

Speaking the Truth in Love

Despite the fact that we have a mandate to speak the truth, Scripture also clearly indicates the attitude with which the mandate is to be accomplished. It is not an attitude of condemnation, but of compassion. We are to speak the truth in *love*. The Greek word here is *agape*, implying that the attitude with which we speak the truth must be an imitation of God's character, expressed in his relationship with his people.

God's love is available to all:

- It expresses itself through ultimate sacrifice (John 3:16).

- It initiates relationship, even with those who seem hostile (Romans 5:8).

- It maintains its hold on us in spite of any calamity (Romans 8:35–39).

- It exceeds our ability to understand (Ephesians 3:18–19).

- Its goal is the reconciliation of relationship with God through Christ (Ephesians 2:4–9).

The human expression of that kind of love can be compared to watering or fertilizing the crops. It gives nutrients required for the crop to thrive. Imagine the impact when someone speaks the truth but does it with the attitude described in 1 Corinthians 13:4–8:

Love (agape) is patient. It doesn't require you to get everything right the first time.

Love is kind. It is compassionate and understanding.

It does not envy, it does not boast, it is not proud. Love does not assume that your sins are worse than mine, and that somehow I come closer to God's ideal than you do.

It is not rude. Love is the embodiment of the Golden Rule: "Do unto others as you would have them do unto you."

It is not self-seeking. Love seeks to grow God's kingdom, not my own.

It is not easily angered. Love doesn't get mad when you disagree with me.

It keeps no record of wrongs. Love doesn't say "I told you so" when you fail. And it doesn't keep a catalog of your sins, pulling out the list occasionally to remind you of your unacceptability. Love is always looking to future possibilities rather than wallowing in past failures.

Love does not delight in evil but rejoices with the truth. Love hates it when you fail, but in response, it sows the seeds for future success. It tells you the truth and holds you accountable for your behavior and your character.

It always protects, always trusts, always hopes, always perseveres. Love always undergirds and supports your efforts to obey God's Word. It always hopes and prays for your success.

Love never fails. Truth spoken in love will always leave a crop well-watered and well-fertilized. It will never fail to bring a healthy harvest of Christian disciples.

Weeds in the Field

A healthy harvest does not imply the absence of weeds. Rice farmers from Northern California understand that very well. Every year they flood their fields and sow their seeds from the air, dropping them from planes. As the rice plants sprout and grow bright green, they often have company—water grass. This weed flourishes in the same conditions as rice. In its early stages, it looks so similar to rice that it is hard to distinguish. It is even harder to exterminate, so farmers let it grow side-by-side with the rice. Water grass develops more rapidly than the crop, towering over and shading the rice plants. It competes for sunlight and nutrients. It drops its seeds before the rice matures, so it always reseeds itself before the farmer can do anything about it.[9]

Obviously, if the farmer could choose optimal conditions, he would eradicate the water grass. He would plant his good and fruitful seed in fields that are completely clean and free of weeds, and he would never have to deal with weed seeds blown in from the neighbor's field. But in a fallen world, those kinds of optimal conditions exist only in fairy tales.

Jesus knew that when he told the parable of a man who sowed good seed in his field and then, apparently satisfied with his work, went home for the evening. While he was sleeping, his enemy came and sowed weeds. No one noticed at first, but "when the wheat sprouted and formed heads, then the weeds also appeared" (Matthew 13:26). The farmer's hired hands told him about the problem, asking if they should pull out all the weeds. "No," the farmer replied, "because while you are pulling the weeds, you may root up the wheat with them. Let both grow together until the harvest. At that time I will tell the harvesters: First collect the weeds and tie them in bundles to be burned; then gather the wheat and bring it into my barn" (Matthew 13:29–30).

In the King James Version, the weeds are called "tares." These little plants, like California's water grass, were almost indistinguishable from the main crop when they first sprouted.

After they developed heads, the difference was clear, but by that time the roots had become intertwined with the wheat. Any attempt to remove them would destroy the main crop.

What Do You Do with the Tares?

The tares described in Scripture are also called "bearded darnel." They are nasty weeds, with semi-poisonous seeds. There are harmful consequences if they are milled and eaten along with the wheat.[10]

Biblical scholar William Barclay tells us the farmer in this story had three choices for dealing with these noxious weeds. Wheat grows much taller than darnel. So, in a badly infested field, the farmer might skim his scythe over the top, harvesting the wheat heads without touching the darnel. Once the harvest was complete, he would burn the entire field to avoid repetition of the same problem. Or sometimes, while he was reaping, the farmer would simply separate the darnel from the wheat, leaving it in bundles to be collected and burned. Often, in a case where there was just a small infestation of darnel, the farmer harvested the whole thing, and then separated the kernels when the grain was milled. Because it was slate-gray, it was easily distinguishable from the grain.[11]

Barclay says this story could have been based on a factual event. He cites Roman laws penalizing people for sowing weeds in someone else's field. He also cites an Eastern story of a man gaining revenge on a neighbor by sowing Kusseb seeds (a kind of reed) in his enemy's garden. The soil was freshly ploughed, so the seed sprouted easily, taking over the entire plot. This man's revenge was realized, for the story concluded, "From that day to this—it is now some ten years—he could not plough a single furrow in it for the mass of Kusseb, and his olive trees withered away."[12]

So, Jesus' verbal picture was not an improbable story. Like all of Jesus' parables, it has a spiritual meaning. Jesus' explanation is recorded in Matthew 13:36–43. He is the sower, the field is the world, and the good seed represents his followers. He plants them in the world. The weeds are people who are not yet part of God's kingdom. Satan is the enemy who plants them in the farmer's field. The harvest refers to the end of the age. It is not the harvest of the evangelistic cycle, but it incorporates some lessons that apply to the principles of this book.

Barclay gives the traditional interpretation; this parable stands as a warning against judging others. Until the fruit comes, we can't distinguish wheat from tares, and even when we can, it is God's job to sort it out. This does not eliminate the need for proper church discipline. Some people we think are weeds, though, may turn out to be fruitful wheat, and others we think are wheat may turn out to be noxious tares. We simply cannot judge that one person deserves to be nurtured and another does not. All people are created in God's image. All people have a right to hear and respond to the gospel. We don't have a right to choose between the wheat and the tares. That is God's job.

Barclay also notes, however, a second possible interpretation. Jesus may have been responding to the disciples' concern regarding the rough people who were surrounding their Master. Relying on traditional wisdom, they may have believed those hoodlums reflected badly on Jesus' Messianic claims. Barclay suggests that Jesus' disciples may have been inwardly complaining, "You say the kingdom has come. But how can that be when we still see so many bad people mixed in with the good?"

Jesus' answer is in the parable. As Barclay phrases it, "No farmer would delay his harvest just because there are some weeds about. He knows there are weeds; there never was a harvest without weeds; and therefore, weeds or no weeds, when the harvest is come he reaps. So then, sinners or no sinners, the kingdom of God is here, and God's reaping is begun."[13]

So What's a Farmer to Do?

If weeds are simply a fact of life, then what are we supposed to do? As with most of the points in this book, the answer has more than one part.

Remember Lessons from the Book's Beginning

The fields, the time, and the harvest all belong to God. He has the right to tell us what to do in every situation. We must stay close to him, keeping our character clean and maintaining our integrity so that our lifestyle is free of things that hinder us from hearing his directions. We will find guidance in his Word and specific direction as we maintain open communication with him, the Lord of the Harvest.

Pray

In her book on intercession, Joy Dawson reminds us, "Prayer proves our dependence on God. All independence is the height of pride, and prayerlessness is a manifestation of unbelief. A life without prayer says, 'I don't need God in this situation, and even if I did pray, what difference would it make?'"[14] Prayer is no less important at this stage of harvest than at any other. Prayer is the plow that breaks through the hardened soil of wearied and worn hearts. It also brings sunshine and gentle showers. It guards against pestilence and disease. Because spiritual harvest is a supernatural process, it requires supernatural resources that are accessed only through petitioning God.

Keep Rebuilding and Maintaining the Soil

Farmer Sidney Chang of South Deerfield, Massachusetts, told journalist Cynthia Vagnetti, that, for him, soil is life. "Everywhere I go," he explained, "I grab some soil, just to feel the texture." Soil, he says, is God's gift. "You've got to take care of it. If all you do is plant vegetables and don't do anything to that soil, after a couple of years, they don't grow. . . .You have to put in what you take out. It's a nice little cycle, and if you maintain it, you can preserve it for years and years."[15] The same principles are true for spiritual harvest, where soil maintenance preserves an environment that encourages growth and discourages weeds and pests. Maintaining the quality of the soil is not a one-time task—it is an on-going process, as we discussed in chapter 7.

Praise God for this Part of the Cycle

Don't allow yourself to become fatigued in this time when responsibility seems unrewarded. Remember Paul's admonition: "Let us not become weary in doing good, for at the proper time we will reap a harvest if we do not give up" (Galatians 5:9). Keep reminding yourself—the work is hard, but harvest is right around the corner.

Sow This Book into Your Life

1. This chapter is based on the ideal of producing disciples, not just converts. Disciples are people who have the desire and ability to reproduce themselves. One pastor from Stittville, New York, told us that, a few years ago, he began considering an important question: "Why should God send us new converts unless we are ready to disciple them?" He noted, "We had experienced a variance of literacy, self learning ability, and

motivation in new believers." That's a common enough observation, but it led this pastor to develop a unique plan. "We felt
they needed to be discipled individually or as couples instead
of in a 'new believers' class," he explained.

So the pastor began mentoring mentors. They, in
turn, mentor new converts and untrained believers. That
is coupled with a requirement that new members take a
discipleship class and a spiritual gifts seminar. After three
years of developing and using this program, the pastor
reports, "This year we have seen growth with new converts
coming to our church and, interestingly, Christians who had
never been grounded in their faith. They say things like, 'I
know I can grow here.'"

This is the essence of "nurturing the crop": developing
a congregation of mature believers with right attitudes and
actions who are capable of reproducing themselves in the
lives of others. Is that reflected in your church? Why or why
not?

_____

_____

_____

_____

_____

2. Based on the information in this chapter, rate your church's
commitment to speaking the truth in love. On the scale below,
circle the number that best fits your church.

　　0　1　2　3　4　5　6　7　8　9　10

Not committed at all ....Totally sold out

3. Now rate your church's *success* in speaking the truth in love.

0   1   2   3   4   5   6   7   8   9   10

Not successful at all ....Totally successful

4. How does your church's commitment and success reveal itself in the quality of the disciples in your congregation?

_____

_____

_____

5. How can you improve?

_____

_____

_____

In preparation for chapter 11, read:

Matthew 9

Leviticus 19:9–10

Deuteronomy 24:19–22

2 Corinthians 6:2

P   A   R   A

chapter 11 < harvest

As I write this chapter, the first real cool front has marched through our neighborhood announcing summer's virtual conclusion. The expansive sky is bright blue, punctuated occasionally by white, cottony clouds. The breeze blowing through my window is tinged with a brisk scent that is unique to autumn. The leaves of early-turning trees are taking on amber and copper hues with the sporadic interruption of scarlet. Flowerbeds are losing their petunias, which are beign replaced with cool-weather chrysanthemums and pansies. Soon the hum of traffic will succumb to the putt-putt-putt of tractors going to and from surrounding fields of cotton, peanuts, soybeans, corn, and wheat. Harvest is literally right around the corner.

The scene will differ from biblical days. This year's harvest in Tidewater, Virginia, will require tractors, reapers, and combines, rather than donkeys and oxen and manpower. It will focus on many crops that weren't even grown in biblical Israel. Yet, in the face of so many differences, the similarities are striking. Harvest will still be the result of several months of hard work; it will offer crucial provision for mankind; and it will occur according to the seasons that God established, as he testified to Noah after the flood (see Genesis 8:22).

The Timeliness of Spiritual Harvest

Despite technological advances, harvest is still a time of tremendous labor because it is a time-sensitive event. It carries a certain vulnerability, which Mona Riley relates in her experience growing carrots in her backyard with her sons, aged four and six. She put extra effort into preparing the soil, and she planted the seeds according to the directions. She carefully tended the tiny plants, defending them from the boys' impatient, questioning fingers. But she made a crucial mistake when the Riley family vacation coincided with the time when the carrots should be harvested. Mona writes:

> We watered carefully the day after our return and then went out to pull our carrots up. Jon bit in first.
>
> "It tastes like wood," he said, his face contorted in disgust. Since Jon had fallen and buried his top front teeth in the backyard retaining wall months before, we figured he knew what he was talking about! But Jared and I both tasted anyway.
>
> "These are awful," Jared agreed.
>
> It was unanimous. "They must have been in the ground too long," I sighed. "Sorry, kids." We washed the carrots and assembled the twenty-pound pile on the patio. We had grown carrots, but they were inedible because we had waited too long to harvest them.[1]

That same factor affects just about any crop. As one agriculturalist explains, "The difference between harvesting an excellent crop and suffering a total loss may well be a matter of hours. . . . The most obvious example of critical time can be seen at harvest, when combines and trucks may have to race furiously against an impending storm with its dark potential of destructive hail." He adds that, even in the best of conditions, "Each day of delay reduces harvest by predictable average amounts."[2]

Spiritual harvest, like agricultural harvest, is a time-sensitive event. A pastor friend recently expressed his ministry frustration like this: "Harvest is hard. You have to time it right, because it really happens just before the fruit rots." The Apostle Paul taught this principle when he quoted Isaiah 49:8: "This is what the LORD says: 'In the time of my favor I will answer you, and in the day of salvation I will help you.'" Paul adds this commentary: "I tell you, now is the time of God's favor, now is the day of salvation" (2 Corinthians 6:2).

The following story from the past tells what happens when Christians leave a spiritual crop too long in its field. After the World War II victory of the Allied Forces, General Douglas MacArthur was named supreme allied commander during the occupation of Japan from 1945 through 1952. He virtually had dictatorial powers over the Japanese people. MacArthur wrote telegrams and letters to various U.S. organizations, earnestly requesting thousands of missionaries and Bibles.

In one letter he explained, "I have publicly stated my firm belief that Christianity offers to Japanese a sure and stable foundation on which to build a democratic nation. Japanese are becoming increasingly aware of fundamental values of Christian religion and appreciate its spiritual and moral blessing. Your assistance will be of inestimable value."[3]

The harvest was ripe, but Western churches failed to respond. Today, only about 2.5 percent of Japan's population claims to be Christian. Harvest—both spiritual and physical—is a time-sensitive event. Because of that, agriculturalists say the quality of farm machinery has the greatest impact at this stage in the agricultural process.

Tractor Development Impacts Harvest

Tractors and combines have long ago replaced horses and

mules, which in turn replaced manpowered sickles. In fact, as one historian relates, "In one generation between 1920 and 1950, most farms in the United States changed from dependence on draft animals to dependence on mechanical power. That change was a profound one."[4]

In 1860, the average American farm worker produced enough food and fiber to feed himself and about five other people. By 1950, productivity had grown so that one farm worker produced enough to feed twenty-five people. Within another quarter-century, that amount had doubled, so that one farm worker produced enough to feed more than fifty people.

The *McGraw-Hill Encyclopedia of Food, Agriculture and Nutrition* tells us, "Mechanization, which allowed each farm worker to increase the area managed, is largely responsible for this dramatic change." A mechanical cotton picker, for instance, will harvest cotton at a rate forty to fifty times that of a hand picker. A peanut harvester turns out about three hundred pounds of shelled peanuts per hour. Doing the same job by hand would require three hundred hours of work.[5] Technology's positive impact is obvious. Fewer and fewer people can produce more and more food. They can do it in a timely manner with less intense labor.

Spiritual Implications

Just as farmers have used technology to improve their yield, evangelists and missionaries have learned to use new methods of travel, communication, and other high-tech advancements to spread the good news of salvation. God has used print media, radio, and TV to efficiently grow his global kingdom. Now the expanding technology of computers has added a new medium so pervasive that some church development consultants encourage churches to hire a staff person simply to manage web sites and promote evangelistic communication in cyberspace. We've seen web churches arise. The beauty of web-based ministry is that it literally knows no geographic or political boundary. Technology has tremendous potential to increase the harvest for God's glory.

I am completely in favor of using any form of media or technological advancement to increase the audience for, or the cultural clarity of, the gospel. God's people have effectively used such innovation throughout history. Sometimes, though, we have used it ineffectively.

A man once visited us at AIMS specifically to question our reason for existence. He said he personally had flown over every country in the world, dropping leaflets that explained salvation; therefore, the work of the Great Commission was finished, and missions agencies like AIMS were no longer needed. But all of those leaflets were written in English: it did not occur to him that the majority of people in those nations could not read them. Technology gives us the ability to do things we never could have envisioned one hundred years ago—and sometimes, it gives us the ability to do them badly.

Beyond that, when we're dealing with technology, even if we use it well, we need to make sure we keep our priorities straight. You see, in the farming world, tractors are useful tools, but harvest can be halted when a tractor breaks down. In the church world, harvest should never be limited by the temporary or permanent failure of "machinery." Technology is a wonderful servant, but it is a lousy master. Western Christians, who have such a plethora of tools, should never succumb to the insidious temptation of relying on the power of the tools more than the power of the Holy Spirit.

The discussion of tools for spiritual harvest in many cultures must include references to technology. But that is just the tip of the iceberg. Throughout the millennia following Christ's sacrificial death, God's people have used a variety of resources to grow his kingdom. The same principle is true today.

Some churches and ministries use door-to-door evangelism programs. Others develop programs for lifestyle evangelism. Still others use small group outreach. The list of strategies could continue indefinitely. "Machinery" can refer to any tool or resource used to bring people to healthy, mature, reproducing relationships with God, through Jesus Christ, in the power of the Holy Spirit. God assigns very big fields to some churches and ministries, and they require big equipment. But the equipment should include *all* the people and resources that a church or ministry can mobilize.

Tractor Lessons

In researching this book, I was surprised to learn that tractors have had impact beyond the realm of farming—and some people question whether the impact was completely positive. I thought about this for a long time, and I have discovered some warnings that apply to our spiritual harvest systems.

Tractors Moved People from Farms to Cities

Throughout human history, technological improvement in farming implements always contributed to urbanization. Going back to biblical days, David C. Hopkins notes, "One finds that the urban revolution was heralded by the invention of the plow, a technological breakthrough" which yielded more food produced by fewer people.[6] The tractor, which had a similar effect on productivity, also had the same effect on the population. Writing about the era right after World War II, an agricultural historian writes, "During that period, most Americans migrated from the farm to the city. The 'why' and 'how' of that movement merit more attention, because an ever-shrinking percentage of the population managed to produce ever-larger quantities of food for the swelling cities. The tractor was a major factor in allowing production to expand while the labor force contracted. It was not the only reason, but it was a major one."[7]

That leads me to the first spiritual lesson. Local churches and ministries cannot afford to develop systems that displace the person in the pew and disengage him or her from the harvest process. We live and work in a world that some describe as suffering from "communal anorexia." Leonard Sweet, in his books dedicated to ministry in contemporary, postmodern culture, tells us, "There is a deepening desire for a life filled with friends, community, service, and creative and spiritual growth. The church must provide its people with a moral code, a vision of what gives life value, and an experience of embeddedness in a community to which one makes valuable contributions. Personal relationships are key in postmodern ministry."[8]

First century Christians turned the known world upside down by developing and evangelizing their networks of personal relationships. That strategy enabled Christians to grow God's kingdom in their own communities. But it worked in the cross-cultural setting as well. The effectiveness of that strategy has never changed. Even in the technology-laden twenty-first century, the most effective spiritual "farm equipment" is still the congregation. We must not alienate our people from the process; instead, we must put tools in their hands and desire in their hearts and watch to see what God will do through them.

Tractors Are Costly

Man-powered sickles and animal-powered harvesters were fueled by the fruit of the farm. Tractors required gasoline, which of course, could not be grown on the farm. This had tremendous impact on agricultural communities all across the United States. Farmers no longer needed to earmark a certain portion of their property (about one-fourth of their total holdings) for raising food for draft animals. Now they could use that property to produce commercial crops.

In fact, agricultural historians tell us that as little as one-half of the increase in crop production for human consumption was directly related to the increased efficiency birthed by the tractor. The other half was only indirectly related, coming from the acres freed from the need to raise food for horses and mules. In 1941, estimates of released land came to about thirty-five million acres that had shifted into market production between 1918 and 1945. Historians tell us that about 16 million horses disappeared in the 1930s. Their replacement by tractors contributed at least partially to the economic depression of that period. You see, as horses disappeared, farmers also lost a valuable market for horse feed.[9]

Second, farmers entered the realm where their need to consume would match or exceed their ability to produce. The high cost of technology put many farmers into overwhelming debt, even as it does today. The first investment is only the beginning. Horses give birth to more horses; tractors give birth to nothing. The investment in a horse yields the possibility of additional development without additional expense. The investment in a tractor inherently requires additional investment for maintenance and replacement. Now the farmer also was dependent on an outside source for fuel.

The second lesson for spiritual harvest is simple. I cannot tell you what kinds of tools will work best in your particular area of ministry. You must develop those in light of God's leading and your research. But I can offer this general suggestion that I think will have incredible impact in your specific situation.

Build a system that is organic rather than organizational. That doesn't mean it will lack organization. No one looking at the organic world that God created could say that it lacks order and consistency. But it also energizes itself, restores itself, rebuilds itself and replaces itself. If you do this like the farmer who harvests by hand with scythes and sickles, or who purchases a draft horse, your system may require an initial investment. In the long-term, however, it will conserve resources lost by fueling, maintaining and replacing a "machine."

The Agribusiness Mentality in Spiritual Harvest

Because of economic realities, contemporary agribusiness bases decisions primarily on financial factors. One author tells us that, especially in the years since World War II, food companies select "crop varieties based on . . . qualities such as uniform ripening, toughness of skin for mechanical harvesting, and tensile strength for shipping. These 'genes of commercial importance' took precedence over those for nutrition and even taste."[10]

What does that mean? One farmer may plant a certain kind of potato because of its uniform dimensions. If all his potatoes are the same size, the labor at harvest-time will be considerably easier and faster because it can be mechanized. Another farmer may choose a specific kind of corn because it all ripens at the same time. He can accomplish his whole harvest at one time instead of having to stagger it. A third farmer may select a certain kind of cucumber because it has tougher skin than another kind. It is more likely to withstand the rigors of shipping.

All of these farmers must consider marketability, as well. In the United States, at least, that is broadly affected by appearance. For instance, certain tomatoes might be considerably higher in vitamin content than others, but because they are yellow rather than red, they are not attractive to the U.S. consumer. Thus, for economic reasons, farmers will plant a crop of less nutritional value. They will plant what they know they can sell with the least amount of effort.

Mona Riley sees a similar value system, unfortunately, among Christians. "Many churches are like pickers in the vineyard," she writes. "Some people are attractive. Maybe they are easier to reach. Whatever our reasons, we pick them and overlook others. What happens to those who are overlooked? Like the leftover clusters of grapes, they are often at the mercy of destructive forces from this world." She adds, "If we are honest, we much prefer well-adjusted, well-employed, healthy, and happy people."[11]

The Ministry of Gleaning

Scripture tells us how the Israelites were to deal with the part of the crop that was, intentionally or unintentionally, left in their fields. Leviticus 19:9–10 demands, "When you reap the harvest of your land, do not reap to the very edges of your field or gather the gleanings of your harvest. Do not go over your vineyard a second time or pick up the grapes that have fallen. Leave them for the poor and the alien. I am the LORD your God." That mandate is restated in more detail in Deuteronomy 24:19–22 and it is described in narrative form in the book of Ruth. The literal application is clear. Those who were caught in the grip of poverty were to benefit from what was left behind in the field.

But what does this mean in contemporary ministry? Well, gleaning is difficult work. "How hard to pick up grain, kernel by kernel by kernel, until there is enough for a meal," Mona Riley explains. "And yet, how valuable the gleaned grain is to those truly hungry! It is difficult to harvest; yet once gathered, it is every bit as useful for food as the first grain which drops on the threshing floor."[12]

There is room in spiritual harvest for those who are called to be gleaners, working among the seemingly less attractive people who don't quite fit our mold. These people may have physical, mental, or emotional disabilities. They may be embroiled in some sin or addiction. They may spew hate and venom. Yet Jesus loves them. He died for them, and they are a viable and valuable part of his harvest.

Second, Scripture specifically records that the laws regarding gleaning were to benefit those who lacked personal power, and those who were aliens. The application is obvious; when you are considering your resources and developing tools for harvest, do not forget those who are most poverty-stricken in a spiritual sense.

In missions circles, we call those people "unreached." They live primarily in regions dominated by religious or political powers that are hostile to the gospel. Usually, they endure unbelievable suffering and poverty. They have little hope, for they are trapped in systems and lifestyles that contribute to their poverty. And they have nothing to look forward to in the next life, for they lean on empty religious promises that have no eternal hope. Statistics indicate that as many as 12 to 13 million of these people die annually, passing into a Christ-less eternity without ever hearing the gospel in a culturally relevant way that they can grasp and apply to their own lives. Many of these people will shout the prophet's lament: "The harvest is passed, the summer has ended, and we are not saved" (Jeremiah 8:20).

The laws related to gleaning, when applied to spiritual harvest, require every believer and every local church to consider the plight of the unreached. Resist the temptation to invest all of your resources in programs that will, in turn, benefit you in some way. "When you reap the harvest of your land, do not reap to the very edges of your field or gather the gleanings of your harvest," Moses wrote on God's behalf. "Do not go over your vineyard a second time or pick up the grapes that have fallen. Leave them for the poor and the alien." The law requires an intentional earmarking of certain resources to benefit the poor and alien.

At AIMS, we suggest an entry-level amount for churches that are willing to obey this mandate in spiritual harvest. We believe a church should set aside at least 10 percent of its total budget for cross-cultural ministry, then grow further with faith promise giving. At least one-fourth of that amount should be dedicated to the world's unreached. We suggest a similar commitment for personnel. We believe a church should strive to see at least 10 percent of its people involved in cross-cultural ministry, with at least one-fourth of them ministering somehow to the unreached. This may be through outreach to international students. It may be through short-term trips, prayer walks, and so on. The way you invest your money and your people will depend on the field God assigns to you and the strategy he gives to bring about his harvest.

Tractor Jobs and Weed Eater Jobs

We can all clearly see that harvest does not happen by accident. A person picking wild blackberries may not have planted the bushes, and he may not have nurtured the crop, but he has to extend the effort to seek them out and pluck them from their thorny environment. He either will eat them on the spot, or he will put them in a container, transport them to another place, and prepare them for eating. Harvest requires effort, and it generally requires some sort of system and tool, which vary according to job requirements.

A friend was driving to work one day when she saw a sign in the median: "Mowing ahead." She expected to see a large tractor with a brush-hog or some other type of mower attached to it. Instead, she saw twenty men hard at work with weed-eaters. She laughed at first, thinking it was a terrible waste of manpower. The job could have been accomplished much more effectively, she thought, with one man driving a big machine.

But when she passed the same spot on the way home that evening, she noticed that twenty men with weed eaters had mowed that median strip very effectively. They had trimmed every blade of grass around the guide rails, which would have been impossible with a large, bulky tractor and mower. The secret to strategically increasing efficiency is not always in getting a bigger tractor. Sometimes it is in enlisting more workers. I think that is almost always true in the realm of spiritual harvest. I am thankful God already told us how to do that.

"Pray to the Lord of the Harvest"

Matthew 9 records part of Jesus' very active ministry. In the events recorded therein, Jesus calls Matthew into ministry. He answers specific questions related to personal discipleship. He heals several people, casts out some demons, and restores life to a dead girl. Scripture summarizes his ministry like this: "Jesus went through all the towns and villages, teaching in their synagogues, preaching the good news of the kingdom and healing every disease and sickness" (Matthew 9:35).

Then the tone changes, for Matthew tells us that, when Jesus saw the vast crowds surrounding him, "he had compassion on them, because they were harassed and helpless, like sheep without a shepherd." In response, Jesus told his disciples, "The harvest is plentiful and the workers are few. Ask the Lord of the harvest, therefore, to send out workers into his harvest field" (Matthew 9:36–38).

The secret to recruitment is prayer. Andrew Murray

explains that, because Jesus had entrusted his disciples with the work of harvest, he also "gives them authority to apply to him for laborers," and he "makes the supply dependent on their prayer." Murray adds, "Without this prayer, fields ready for reaping will be left to perish."[13]

We must ardently seek God's guidance as we develop the system and the tools that will work best in the fields he has assigned. We also must pray for workers. And frankly, we needn't be gentle in our prayers. Our English translation says we are to ask God to "send out" workers. But the Greek is stronger. It uses the word *ekballo,* which means "to eject, to cast out, or to expel."[14] It's the same term used to refer to Jesus' casting out demons. Harvest is on God's heart, and he is willing to go to great lengths to provide the laborers needed. We must simply ask.

Sow This Book into Your Life

1. This chapter suggests building a harvest system that is organic rather than organizational. It explains that an organic system energizes itself, restores itself, rebuilds itself, and re-places itself. Describe what that would look like in a church or ministry setting. How can you tell if your church or ministry is organic or organizational?

_____

_____

_____

2. This chapter also discusses the importance of your harvest machinery. A senior pastor in North Carolina explained that he sees churches as "storehouses or supply quarters." He said a local church is the spiritual equivalent of Future Farmers of

America, only it is supposed to cultivate the world. He added that his church has a "harvest-sized vision," and they are somewhere in the middle of the process. "We've plucked a few ears of corn so far," he wrote, adding that the long-term goal is to have a harvest so big that it requires "a combine." We love the way he worded that.

• Respond to that word picture. In light of the material presented in this chapter, describe your church's harvest machinery.

_____

_____

_____

• How does that reality affect your goals for present and future harvest?

_____

_____

• How can you correct any deficiencies that you find?

_____

_____

3. A pastor from an outreach in Virginia told us, "I grew up on a farm. The whole process of farming was important, however, the *harvest* was critical. You would do whatever it took to bring the harvest in. The question is, what are we willing to do to save the harvest?" How would you answer that question?

_____

_____

_____

P A R A

In preparation for chapter 12, read:

Isaiah 28 (You read it for another chapter, but a re-reading will help prepare you for chapter 12.)

Psalm 139

Psalm 30

S ir Robert Watson-Watt was one of Great Britain's World War II heroes. He isn't remembered for flying or navigating or shooting—he's remembered for inventing radar, which helped the Royal Air Force to be consistently in the right place at the right time to meet the challenge of German Luftwaffe aircraft during the Battle of Britain, August through October of 1940. For his contribution, Watson-Watt received fifty thousand pounds from the British government. He also received the U.S. Medal of Merit.[1]

Several years later, after he moved to Canada, Watson-Watt was arrested for speeding. Ironically, he was caught in a radar trap. In response, he wrote this poem:

Pity Sir Robert Watson-Watt,
Strange target of his radar plot,
And thus, with others I could mention,
A victim of his own invention.[2]

Obviously, this is not an agricultural story, but it does illustrate a Scriptural point that has its roots in the agricultural mindset. Robert Watson-Watt reaped what he sowed—and as noted in previous chapters, that is always true. In biblical days, it was equally true that you *sowed* what you reap.

You Reap What You Sow, and You Sow What You Reap

Today's agricultural reality generally involves seed catalogs and companies. A few hearty gardeners still harvest seeds for replanting, but most rely on outside sources. That hasn't always been true. In fact, in the broad scope of agricultural history, it hasn't been true for very long.

Louise Eubank Gray recalls growing up on a Virginia farm in the early 1900s, noting, "A farmer usually planted corn from his own seed kept from the previous year. Sometimes he might buy a different variety from a neighbor, if he wanted to experiment a little."

Louise describes the process:

Uncle Combs climbed with some difficulty into the grain barn, seated himself on an overturned bucket, and began to pick through a large heap of corn. Seed corn was taken from the best ears, large, well-filled ones from the previous year's crop. Throwing to one side small or poorly shaped ears, he soon had a pile of selects before him. Next he shelled the small grains from the tips of the ears, his dark hands rubbing the dry kernels from the cobs easily, and threw them into a small bucket. At last he was ready to shell the seed corn into a half-bushel measure held between his knees.[3]

That picture is similar to the process a farmer would have employed in biblical days. Harvest, of course, provided food for man and beast alike. But, as noted earlier, harvest ended one agricultural cycle and began the next. Farmers saved seed for the next crop.

In the realm of spiritual harvest, we must come to terms with this basic concept. Harvest is not just for our own spiritual storing, feasting, and celebration. While feasting and celebrating are valid responses to God's victorious expansion of his kingdom, we must not pursue converts just so we can count them and keep them in church. We disciple them and teach them to reinvest their lives in future harvest.

Reinvesting Spiritual Seed

Many years ago, E. Stanley Jones, Methodist missionary to India, noted, "The conception of one half of the world saved, and the other half lost, the half that is saved going out after the half lost, is a misconception. . . . In the days to come we shall want these men whose hearts have been touched with the grace of God to come and help us in the uncompleted task of evangelization."[4] I've built my entire ministry on this type of understanding. And by God's grace, AIMS is seeing this happen all over the world. Here is one example.

In July 2002, in partnership with ministries in Mexico, AIMS presented its first-ever completely Spanish *Harvest Connection Seminar.* AIMS designed this missions mobilization tool to adapt to any culture through language translation. This seminar covers major aspects of missions mobilization, including the need to raise up personnel and also to support them financially. The thought of making this financial investment can be a major leap for Christians in developing countries, but we demonstrate mathematically that they can support missionaries without relying on outside help. Our goal is to lead them to depend on God's provision rather than on foreign funds. In nearly every venue, this presentation births great excitement.

Mexico City was no exception. One of the leaders who attended this event told the AIMS presenter that starting the very next day, his church would earmark 5 percent of their budget for cross-cultural ministry, and they would work to increase the amount. This man was senior pastor at a church of about eight hundred people, and he has now reconfigured his entire ministry with a view toward global harvest. He is making an incredible personal investment, leaving his church in capable hands and moving to a strategic field in Eastern Europe.

This man's experience is multiplied daily throughout the world. AIMS works with denominations and church networks throughout Latin America, Africa, and Asia. These places, once considered mission fields, are now raising up and sending missionaries into other cultures. This is the cross-cultural application of the harvest mentality—reinvesting seed for future yield. But where does it begin?

Revival Must Proceed with a Harvest Mentality

Revival is one of those Christian catchwords that is hard to define. We know it implies a certain spiritual rejuvenation—a return to the emotional and spiritual fervor evident when a person first meets Christ. Charles Finney, the great Christian spokesman of the nineteenth century, said that revival "presupposes that the Church is sunk down in a backslidden state," and it "consists in the return of the Church from her backslidings and the conversion of sinners." In essence, he explained, "Revival is a new beginning of obedience with God."[5]

But Finney also believed that, when churches are reformed through revival's purifying influence, the end result would be the salvation of people who have never responded to the gospel.

Unfortunately, this is not always the case. Too often revival becomes an in-grown celebration of God's blessing. Joyous celebration is a natural response to God's intervention among his people. But when the celebration becomes our primary focus, we tend to forget about the outside world. Or, in the aftermath of the emotional response to the visible outpouring of God's Holy Spirit among repentant saints, we become embroiled in theological discussions that impede the gospel's advance.

We see this even in the great Reformation, initiated in large part on October 31, 1517, when Martin Luther nailed his "Ninety-Five Theses Concerning Indulgences" to a door at Germany's University of Wittenberg. Though many others helped bring reformation to other regions, Luther is generally credited with starting the whole process.

While the Reformation played a crucial role in purifying the church, and while it launched Protestantism, it did very little to propel any ongoing reinvestment of resources into God's global harvest. In fact, Ruth A. Tucker's book *From Jerusalem to Irian Jaya*, a standard text on missions history, notes very plainly, "World-wide missions was not a major concern of most of the Reformers." They were busy "just holding their own in the face of Roman Catholic opposition." Protestants had some practical hurdles in their access to travel at that time. But the newfound Protestant theology "was another factor that limited the vision of missionary enterprises."

Tucker explains that Martin Luther was so convinced Christ's return was on the immediate horizon, he overlooked the need for global evangelization. Furthermore, he cemented his position by claiming the Great Commission "was binding only on the New Testament apostles who had fulfilled their obligation by spreading the gospel throughout the known world, thus exempting succeeding generations from responsibility." Although Calvin was the most missionary-minded of the reformers, his doctrine of election seemed to many people to nullify the need for missionary outreach, since "God had already chosen those he would save."[6]

Tucker tells us it wasn't until the eighteenth century—two hundred years after the Reformation's birth—that Protestants made their "first great thrust" into missions, "for it was only then that Protestants in any significant numbers began recognizing their responsibility in evangelizing those without the gospel."[7] It is perhaps significant that this advance began with the Lutherans, finally bringing the movement begun by Martin Luther to the place of reinvesting revival's resources back into global spiritual harvest.

The Ministry of Saving Seed

To avoid hoarding revival's blessings, let's look at lessons learned from those who still harvest physical seeds from their own crops, reinvesting them in the soil and thus continuing the harvest cycle. Admittedly, some of this chapter reviews principles covered elsewhere in this book, but it's an important review.

Use Strong, Healthy Plants

Agriculturalists say you should collect seeds only from strong, healthy plants. In fact, some say you should deliberately let your healthiest, strongest plants mature to the point that they go to seed (as with vegetables like lettuce or broccoli), rather than harvesting them for consumption. By selecting seeds from the best plants, you reduce the chance of passing on undesirable traits to future generations.[8]

My experience indicates that many churches do the opposite. They consume their best resources, rather than investing them for future gain in God's kingdom. They invest large sums of money to erect and maintain ornate buildings. They find their most gifted people and tie up their time and energy in ministry to other Christians. They assign their best teachers to their most mature believers. On the surface, it makes sense. They need a place for the congregation to meet, and mature Christians need to be challenged with material they haven't already heard. But the end result is that evangelism and missions usually get the leftovers.

In response to this trend, one missions agency president wrote, "It's common knowledge that most American Christians—even those in churches that are strong on missions—hold a stereotype of the typical missionary as a well-intentioned but somewhat naïve person of limited ability who probably could not hold down a good job in the home country. The stereotype is unfair, but there are enough missionaries like that to reinforce the image of mediocrity."[9]

I am not denying the legitimacy of housing and feeding a congregation. I am simply saying that, in the agricultural model, harvest has a two-fold purpose: feeding and replanting. Within that context, the part of the crop that is destined for food is primarily intended to *fuel the harvesters*. The other portion is specifically set apart for multiplication through *replanting*. So, whether you are in the portion that is set aside for "feed" or for "seed," your ultimate purpose is the same: to be involved in harvest.

Choose Future Productivity Over Present Attractiveness

If you want to encourage lots of brilliant blooms when you grow flowers, you snip off the flower heads once they begin to wilt. Called "deadheading," this encourages the plant to produce more flowers. But if you want to save seeds, you leave the flowers on the stem even after they die. They might not be as pretty, but as one gardener explains, "The plant will start putting its resources into producing seed instead of new flowers."[10]

A seed saver must choose the long-term goal over short-term success. Similarly, a church or ministry must choose long-term fruitfulness over short-term appearance. Investing your time, energy, and resources in growing seeds instead of flowers implies, of course, that you must let the flower or fruit grow to full maturity. One garden magazine noted "If you cut it off too soon, you might as well throw it away."[11] You have cut off the embryo before it has developed sufficiently to support reproduction.

True scriptural discipleship inherently breeds a desire and ability to reproduce. In keeping with the agricultural paradigm, that should be the natural result of maturity. Yet many churches limit their discipleship program to issues related to personal spirituality, ignoring issues related to evangelism and missions. Church growth specialists Win and Charles Arn discuss that view as follows:

> Today 'discipling' has evolved to mean the process of spiritual perfecting—tutoring, learning, growing, maturing. Few discipling programs in churches today accurately reflect Christ's vision to make disciples or are measured for success on the basis of new disciples produced. While the concept of spiritual maturation is unquestionably important, an exclusive emphasis on spiritual growth often serves as an undesirable magnet, pulling a Christian's focus increasingly inward as concern for those outside the body of Christ progressively decreases. In such a self-centered environment, the goal of fulfilling the Lord's Great Commission moves lower and lower as a priority. [12]

The agricultural mandate requires Christian leaders to recognize the desire for spiritual reproduction as a defining factor of true maturity.

Clean the Seeds

The successful gardener will clean the seeds before storing or planting them. One article suggests using a hairdryer or fan to winnow the seeds—that means separating them from the chaff that surrounds them. As the wind blows over the seeds, the lighter stalks and hulls blow away, leaving only the fruitful part of the seed.[13]

The spiritual application is clear. Even mature believers, interested in and prepared for spiritual reproduction, must go through a purifying process. In the physical realm, the process of cleaning seed for replanting is similar to the initial process of cleaning seed for food.

Threshing and Winnowing

Since Scripture grew from an agricultural society, biblical references to threshing and winnowing are numerous. Biblical farmers did not have our technological advantage, still they creatively discovered how to separate the seed from the chaff, or the waste.

First, the farmer would spread the stalks of grain on a threshing floor, basically a slab of flat rock. He could hitch his oxen to a threshing sledge, a heavy board with stone or metal spikes to break the heads of grain from the stalks; he could force the oxen to walk around on the stalks, or he could beat the stalks with heavy sticks. Then he would use a large wooden fork to toss the stalks into the air. The breeze would carry the lighter chaff to the side, while the heavier grain would fall directly downward into a pile to be gathered for later use. This second step was called winnowing.[14]

Because threshing and winnowing provide basic agricultural metaphors for separating the useful from the non-useful, these processes became word pictures for God's judgment. Only rarely is threshing used as a positive metaphor. (See, for instance, Joel 2:24ff.) Yet, in the agricultural community, the seasons of threshing and winnowing brought joyous celebrations. Why? Because the farmers weren't looking at the process—they were looking at the result. Cleaning the harvest made it both edible and productive.

Threshing God's Way

Referring to a passage in Isaiah 28, Charles Spurgeon laid out some principles of threshing which apply to God's care for his children. We dealt with the first part of this passage in chapter eight, where we discussed the principle of matching seed to soil. Spurgeon concentrated on the end of this passage: "Caraway is not threshed with a sledge, nor is a cartwheel rolled over cumin; caraway is beaten out with a rod, and cumin with a stick. Grain must be ground to make bread; so one does not go on threshing it forever. Though he drives the wheels of his threshing cart over it, his horses do not grind it. All this also comes from the LORD Almighty, wonderful in counsel and magnificent in wisdom" (Isaiah 28:27–29).

So far in this book, we have examined the external spiritual ecosystem in agricultural terms. Now, we will look at the individual believer's internal ecosystem. Spurgeon outlines three major points in this passage, as it relates to God's process of purifying men.[15]

Every Human Needs to Go through This Process

"The best of men are men at best," Spurgeon notes, "and being men, they are not perfect. . . . About the best of men there is still a measure of chaff. . . . Now, threshing is useful in loosening the connection between the good corn and the husk."

He explains that God's threshing "is used to loosen our hold of earthly things and break us away from evil. This needs a divine hand, and nothing but the grace of God can make the threshing effectual. Something is done by threshing when the soul ceases to be bound up with its sin, and sin is no longer pleasurable or satisfactory."

God's Threshing Is Done with Great Discretion

God knows us as individuals, and he chooses the threshing process to fit our specific needs. For some, Spurgeon says, God may use financial setbacks. For others, physical discomfort, or perhaps a strained or lost relationship. God chooses the tool, the time, and the place for separating the seed of our lives from the chaff. At the same time, Spurgeon reminds us, "The husbandman is zealous to beat out the seed, but he is careful not to break it in pieces by too severe a process."

Threshing Will Not Last Forever

When God has achieved his purpose, he will end the process. Though Spurgeon does not specifically say this, his statement implies that, as we cooperate with God, our voluntary obedience and prayer can effectually hasten our purification.

God Threshes Groups As Well As Individuals

God's threshing is not limited to individuals. He sometimes purifies local churches, ministries, and even the Church at large. In the realm of global evangelization Christians have a habit of getting comfortable in their own cultures, settling in, and ignoring the rest of the world. Ralph Winter says this scenario is played out in all of church history. God often threshes or winnows placid believers, allowing them to endure persecution so they scatter to other regions, evangelizing as they go.

Referring to one particular era of persecution, the Viking onslaught against the Roman Empire (about 800 AD), Winter describes the example set by monks and servant girls who were taken prisoner. These hapless captives became cross-cultural evangelists and disciplers, transforming many pagans through their words and deeds. Winter wrote that, from God's viewpoint, the redemption of the Viking conquerors "must have been more important than the harrowing tragedy of this new invasion of Barbarian violence and evil which fell upon God's people whom he loved." [16]

So, how do we cooperate with God in his corporate winnowing process? The same way we cooperate as individuals. To the best of our ability, we voluntarily obey and pray.

How Should We Pray?

We have already discussed the role of prayer in bringing revival. Perhaps that link is enhanced by the fact that true prayer begins by changing the pray-er. That is part of the process of cooperating with God. The Psalmist invites God to "Search me, . . . and know my heart; test me and know my anxious thoughts. See if there is any offensive way in me, and lead me in the way everlasting" (Psalm 139:23–24). That is an example of submissive cooperation.

Griffith John must have been that kind of pray-er. This Welsh missionary, who arrived in China in 1855, once explained, "I long to be filled with divine knowledge, divine wisdom, divine love, divine holiness, to the utmost extent of my capacity. I want to feel that all the currents of my soul are interfused in one channel deep and wide, and all flowing towards the heart of Christ."

In agricultural terms, Griffith John was asking God to

thresh and winnow him. He intentionally asked God to separate him from sin and self, because he wanted to maximize his spiritual harvest. Griffith John knew the first century apostles' success was not determined by their own effort but by Christ's working through them. "They saw with the eyes of Christ, felt with his heart, and worked with his energies," he said. "They were nothing; Christ was everything. Christ was living, breathing, and triumphing in their personal lives. Their entire nature being replete with his life, their spirits bathed in his light, and their souls kindled with the fires of his love, they moved in the midst of men as embodiments of supernatural power." He concluded, "Brethren, this is what we must be, if this mighty empire (China) is to be moved through us."[17]

If that is our goal for the spiritual fields where God has placed us, we must learn to reinvest our harvest for future fruitfulness. We also must refuse to shrink from the purification of spiritual threshing and winnowing. Just as in biblical days, the end result will be joyous celebration, for Scripture promises that, while God's discipline lasts for a moment, "his favor lasts a lifetime." Furthermore, it says, "Weeping may remain for a night, but rejoicing comes in the morning" (Psalm 30:5). From the biblical, agricultural model, we can expect fruitfulness to follow.

Sow This Book into Your Life

1. In biblical days, agricultural success depended not just on harvesting a crop for food but on harvesting seeds for on-going reproduction. As this chapter says, "In the agricultural model, harvest has a two-fold purpose: feeding and replanting. Within that context, the part of the crop that is destined for food is primarily intended to *fuel the harvesters*. The other portion is

specifically set aside for multiplication through *replanting*. So whether you are in the portion that is set aside for 'feed' or for 'seed,' your ultimate purpose is the same: to be involved in harvest."

In many ways, our culture no longer views harvest as the premier focus of life. Have we also lost that focus in the church, as it relates to spiritual harvest? Explain your answer.

_____

_____

_____

_____

2. Review the principles covered under "The Ministry of Saving Seed."

- Collect seeds from strong, healthy plants.
- Choose future productivity over present attractiveness.
- Clean seeds before storing or planting.

Describe how you see those principles already reflected in your church's overall program.

_____

_____

_____

Where do you need to improve? How can those principles help you as you make decisions regarding your church's or ministry's overall program?

_____

_____

_____

3. How have you seen threshing and winnowing take place, not just in individual lives, but in your congregation as a whole? What has been the result?

_____

_____

_____

4. How will your personal and corporate prayers change, based on this book in general and this chapter in particular?

_____

_____

_____

In preparation for chapter 13, read:

John 15

Habakkuk 3:17–19

1 Corinthians 3:6–8

James 5:16–17

P   A   R   A

chapter 13 < fruit that remains

A n American pastor was sent to Korea for two months to research missionary outreach. Since he knew no Korean and the Koreans knew only a little English, there was a distinct language barrier. Still, he had a marvelous time. After he submitted his denominational report, he also sent a thank you note to his hosts. He closed the letter saying, "I hope that God will preserve you and your people."

Several weeks later he got a friendly reply that ended like this. "Thank you for your kind sentiments. I hope that God will pickle you and your people, too."[1]

Every missionary has a similar story about a cultural indiscretion or a gaffe. This one, however, hits closer to home than many of us would like to admit.

You see, Jesus told His disciples, "You did not choose me, but I chose you and appointed you to go and bear fruit—fruit that will last" (John 15:16). In the King James Version, that last phrase is translated, "that your fruit should remain." In practical application, we find ways to preserve our harvest for our own consumption, but Jesus meant something very different when he talked about "fruit that will last." Most of us know Jesus didn't have in mind some type of spiritual pickling and/or canning process.

The Context

Have you noticed that you say the most important things when you are about to leave? Sure, there are mundane reminders of tasks to be done. "Don't forget to put the trash out on Friday." Or, "Make sure you water the plants and pick up the mail." But there is also, "I love you." And, "Drive carefully." And, "Call me when you get there."

Think back to the time when Jesus was leaving his disciples. How important were his last words? That is the context for this verse. It falls within John's record of Jesus' last night before his crucifixion. The Messiah had eaten the Passover dinner. He had washed his disciples' feet. He had explained that one of them would betray him. He had told them he would die. He was preparing them for coming hardships. His words were significant, for they held the truths he wanted them to remember.

Jesus' words were intended primarily for his disciples' consolation. But at the beginning of John 15, we see a shift in language as Jesus emphasizes his desire for his disciples to be productive. "I am the true vine," he explains, "and my Father is the gardener." That sentence begins a parable through which Jesus explains kingdom fruitfulness.

Jesus uses the analogy of a grapevine. He is the vine, the trunk that gives life to the rest of the plant. His Father is the vinedresser or husbandman. He doesn't just care for the vineyard—he owns it. He is vitally interested in its fruitfulness. Jesus' followers are the branches, the shoots coming from the central vine. The life, growth, and development of the shoots and their fruit depend on vital union with the vine.

The application is obvious: Jesus calls his followers to stay connected. (Some translations say, "Abide in me."

Others say, "Remain in me." Still others say, "Maintain a living communion with me."[2]) If that happens, the branch will bear much fruit (verse 5), and the fruit will last (verse 16). We are not talking about here-today-gone-tomorrow fruit. We are talking about fruit that endures, stands the test of time, and proves to be permanent. The verses between 5 and 16 explain how that happens.

Abide, Abide, Abide . . .

In verses 6–15, Jesus uses some form of the Greek verb *meno* (translated *abide, remain,* or *continue*)[3], no less than seven times. It is safe to say he intentionally emphasizes this concept.

He calls his followers to *abide* in him. He tells them his Word must *remain* in them. He says they must *continue* in his love and in God's love. He promises that, as abiding in him is reflected in how we respond to other relationships, the natural result will be abundant fruitfulness.

The implication for Christian leaders is obvious: we must abide in Christ, and we must teach those under our influence to abide in Christ. Fruitfulness, like every other spiritual success, depends on our staying connected with him. Staying connected with him begins with Bible study and prayer, but it also includes listening, meditating, and all the other activities that enhance communion with the Lord of the universe. If we focus our attention and energy on the desired fruit rather than on the Lord of Harvest, we may see limited results, but we will never break through to the abundance God has in mind for every believer and every group of believers.

As James Hudson Taylor once said, "The branch of the vine does not worry, and toil, and rush here to seek for sunshine, and there to find rain. No; it rests in union and communion with the vine; and at the right time, and in the right way, is the right fruit found on it. Let us so abide in the Lord Jesus."[4] *Abiding* is the foundation for *abundance*.

Submit to God's Pruning

The passage shows God, the vinedresser, examining each branch. He knows which ones produce no fruit, a little fruit, or a lot of fruit. Based on that knowledge, he begins pruning.

Bruce Wilkinson's book *Secrets of the Vine: Breaking Through to Abundance* records his early spring move to the country. His new neighbor had a grape vine on the property line, and Wilkinson eagerly anticipated his share of the harvest. One day he saw the man hacking down the entire row. He explains, "My neighbor, a large, white-haired man in overalls, wielded the biggest set of shears I'd ever seen. All around him lay heaps of grape branches."

Wilkinson was understandably appalled, and he went to the fence to discuss the situation. Upon hearing his concerns, the neighbor asked, "You're a city boy, aren't ya? . . . Don't know much about grapes, do ya?" Then the wise man explained, "We can either grow ourselves a lot of beautiful leaves filling up this whole fence line. Or we can have the biggest, juiciest, sweetest grapes you and your family have ever seen. . . . We just can't have both."[5]

Wilkinson writes, "Left to itself, a grape plant will always favor new growth over more grapes. The result? From a distance, luxurious growth, an impressive achievement. Up close, an underwhelming harvest. That's why the vinedresser cuts away unnecessary shoots, no matter how vigorous, because a vineyard's only purpose is . . . grapes. In fact, pruning is a grower's single most important technique for ensuring plentiful harvest."[6]

Wilkinson makes apt applications to the individual Christian, noting that in pruning a vinedresser considers four specific factors: 1) to remove dead branches; 2) to remove branches that shade developing fruit, thus allowing the sunshine to fall on the grapes; 3) to increase the size and sweetness of the fruit; 4) to encourage new development.

God follows similar principles in pruning individual Christians. "To make room for the kind of abundance he created us for, he must first cut away parts of our lives that drain precious time and energy from what's truly important." Wilkinson adds, "In pruning, God asks you to let go of things that keep you from his kingdom purposes and your ultimate good." He adds, "God isn't trying to just take away; he's faithfully at work to make room to add strength, productivity, and spiritual power to your life."[7]

In several places in this book, we've talked about spiritual applications that seem similar to pruning. In chapter seven we noted that composting involves dying to negative behaviors and attitudes that are clearly discussed in Scripture and generally apply to all believers. In chapter twelve we discussed the need to thresh and winnow seeds to prepare them for eating or for planting. Pruning is a similar spiritual concept, but it may have more specific application to an individual. Pruning requires the believer to allow God to cut away things that compete with or distract from fruitfulness, even if those things are not inherently bad. In other words, submitting to God's pruning means that we choose what is best over what is good.

That is easy to see for the individual Christian, but what about a whole group? Why and how does God prune a church or ministry? He works in a similar way. He wants to prune away the extras—the dead wood and leaves that limit our corporate fruitfulness. He wants to take us to a new level of abundance. So, if we are following his plan, we must submit to his pruning. The local church or ministry should have no sacred cows. Every program is subject to cutting if it impedes or interferes with fruitful harvest. That requires that we cultivate attitudes and values that recognize God's place as Lord of our lives and of our ministries.

Let God Be God

A friend served his first pastorate in a retirement community in Florida. Being young and zealous, he invested time and energy trying to achieve the glorious vision of successful ministry instilled in him at seminary. But on occasion, he came dangerously close to defeat, simply because he took on too much. He laughingly told of an older deacon who would call him on the phone. Without any introduction or pretense, the man would simply say, "Pastor, let God be God," and he would hang up.

With four words, that man summarized the fundamental concept that undergirds our entire Christian walk, including harvest. I saw a T-shirt the other day that caught my attention. On the front it said, "There is a God . . ." On the back it said, "and you're not him." Even while I was laughing, I thought seriously about the statement.

In the harvest cycle, many factors are outside our control, but they are not out of God's reach. That brings us back to the beginning of this book. God alone is Lord of the land. He alone is Lord of the time. And he alone is Lord of the harvest. Abiding means we recognize his place. We submit to his ultimate authority. In practicality, that will have at least two results.

Don't Try to Take God's Place

In the physical world, it is easy to see the factors that are purely under God's control. Man has no ability to control the weather or to change the seasons. Man has no ability to make a seed. Similarly, in spiritual harvest, we cannot control circumstances to make them more conducive to harvest. Scripture tells us that is God's job. The Holy Spirit brings conviction (see John 16:7–11). The Father draws people to Jesus (see John 6:44). Jesus saves people and pulls them from Satan's grasp (see John 14:6).

Most of us accept these theological truths intellectually. Yet, in working out a strategy that will lead to spiritual harvest, we may try to assume the role that belongs to God alone. Strategic manipulation is one of the subtle traps. One author, Selwyn Hughes, explains, "Persuasion is the attempt . . . to convince others that our convictions are true and worthy of acceptance. Manipulation is an attempt to persuade . . . in a way that restricts their freedom to reject our appeal." He writes, "We must do all we can to bring people to Christ, but there is a point where we must hold back, for any attempt to persuade someone to accept salvation in a way that restricts their freedom to choose for or against Christ is wrong."[8]

He adds, "We are in danger of manipulating people when we see them simply as souls to be won and have lost sight of their rights as persons. There are some Christians who are more concerned about getting another spiritual 'scalp' than they are for the welfare of the ones to whom they witness. And this is not just a problem in individual witness; it is a problem in mass evangelism too."[9]

This author is not abandoning evangelism and missions. He simply says we shouldn't overstep and try to take God's place, which leads me to the second part of the equation.

Obediently Accept God's Plan for Participation

The harvest mentality requires a delicate balance between trusting and working. We accept God's place as Lord, and we submit to his authority. We also accept our responsibility to steward resources into fruitfulness in every area where we have influence. That includes:

- Clearing the land
- Preparing the soil
- Matching the seed to the soil
- Sowing the seed
- Cultivating the crop
- Harvesting the crop
- Preparing it for future use

I won't review all of those areas except to note that God ordained our involvement. He assigned us a valuable role in his plan to grow his kingdom, and our obedience can affect the eternal destiny of millions. I'll close with three suggestions to help us all live in the tension of investing our lives in the harvest process, even while we trust God and look to him for the outcome.

Be Patient

Every kind of seed has a different germination period. Bean seeds sprout and grow almost over night. That is why they are the prime choice for preschool projects. Children want to see immediate results.

American southerners know about kudzu. Imported from Japan, this quick-growing vine has earned nicknames like the "mile-a-minute-vine" or the "drop-it-and-run-vine." Southern folklore claims it can grow a foot a day in the summer, accumulating sixty feet of growth per year.

And there is the agricultural lore that surrounds corn. Some farmers claim it develops so fast, if you are really quiet on a still summer day, you can hear it growing.

Not all seeds germinate or grow that quickly. Some require a very, very long time to sprout and grow. The farmer who grows bamboo plants the seeds. He will water and fertilize them for as long as four years before he sees any visible results. Then the bamboo plant will finally sprout and grow, and it will become a picture of abundance, spurting up to ninety feet in nine weeks. Why? Because for all those years, the root system has been growing down and out, preparing for the eventual need for water and nutrients to support such rapid growth.

Leonard Sweet makes this application: "The apostle Paul had a Chinese bamboo grass ministry. His first labors were so uneventful in converts and results that it was very easy to overlook the small shoots. But the seeds Paul planted others watered and nurtured until the sprouts of Christianity spread like kudzu throughout the ancient Greek and Roman worlds."[10]

What if sometime in his lengthy wait, the farmer grew weary of caring for the bamboo seed? He would never have seen the fruit of his labor. So let God be God—he made the seed, and he knows when it will sprout. In the meantime, be faithful to do your part. And be patient.

While You Are Waiting, Rejoice

In the face of agricultural failure, the Old Testament prophet Habakkuk committed himself to a specific attitude and action. He described a situation where "the fig tree does not bud and there are no grapes on the vines, . . . the olive crop fails and the fields produce no food." Despite total loss, Habakkuk proclaimed, "I will rejoice in the LORD, I will be joyful in God my Savior" (Habakkuk 3:17–19).

Habakkuk was not talking about a wringing-of-the-hands celebration that hides a gnawing fear that God does not really know what he is doing. The word translated "rejoice" is the Hebrew word *alaz*, which means "to jump for joy." And the word translated "be joyful" is from the root word *guwl*, which means "to spin around under the influence of violent emotion, usually joy."[11] This kind of expression, especially in the shadow of apparent failure, can only grow from the root of understanding who God is and who we are.

The apostle Paul explained it this way: "I planted the seed, Apollos watered it, *but God made it grow*. So, neither he who plants nor he who waters is anything, but only God, who makes things grow. The man who plants and the man who waters have one purpose, and each will be rewarded according to his own labor. For we are God's fellow workers." (1 Corinthians 3:6–8, italics added). God calls his people to faithfulness—not to results. Rejoice! The burden is on God's shoulders, not yours.

Pray Hard

The Old Testament tells of Elijah, God's prophet who confronted Israel's idolatry. Elijah had the uncomfortable task of relaying the message that because the king had led God's people into sin, God would judge them with a lengthy drought. After more than three years of devastation, God told Elijah to confront the king and his false prophets again. The result was the legendary face-off on Mount Carmel when the

Baal worshipers failed to invoke fire from heaven to burn up their sacrifice, but Elijah's God responded with a blaze that burned up the sacrifice, the altar, and even the water and dust around it.

After that, Elijah climbed the mountain and knelt before the Lord. He prayed for rain to end the drought. Six times he sent his servant to look, and six times the servant returned saying, "There is nothing there." Elijah kept praying; the seventh time, the report was different. The servant told him, "A cloud as small as a man's hand is rising from the sea" (I Kings 18:44). That was God's answer. Soon, "the sky grew black with clouds, the wind rose, a heavy rain came on." (I Kings 18:45).

The New Testament summarizes that story in just a few lines. "The prayer of a righteous man is powerful and effective. Elijah was a man just like us. He prayed earnestly that it would not rain, and it did not rain on the land for three and a half years. Again he prayed, and the heavens gave rain, and the earth produced its crops" (James 5:16–18).

D. L. Moody, the great revivalist, applied this understanding of the importance of prayer to the needs for spiritual harvest as readily as Elijah did to the needs for physical harvest. R. A. Torrey, claiming to be Moody's intimate acquaintance, noted, "He was a far greater pray-er than he was preacher."[12] Moody preached, and God brought thousands of people into the kingdom, but Moody's success did not lie in eloquence. It rested on his commitment to prayer.

Elijah demonstrated that God can hold back or release physical rain. He is just as capable of holding back or releasing spiritual blessing. At every step, prayer produces the factors leading to abundant fruitfulness. God's followers must be people of prayer—individually and corporately.

Go Back to the "Root"

A Walk in the Clouds,[13] one of the most beautifully filmed movies I've ever seen, tells the story of a young G.I. who, on returning from World War II, finds he has little in common with the woman he married in haste before he left. Disillusioned, they separate. He heads north to work as a traveling chocolate salesman. On a bus, he meets the daughter of a wealthy vineyard owner. On her way home from college, she is terrified to face her family, for she must tell them she is pregnant and unwed.

The young man, played by Keanu Reeves, graciously offers to pose as her husband for one night, which stretches into many. During his stay, this G.I. learns a lesson that has implications for us. Toward the middle of the movie, the girl's grandfather takes Reeves to see a special vine in the vast vineyard. The old man, played by Anthony Quinn, explains that in 1580, his ancestor came from Spain to Mexico "with a dream in his head, the clothes on his back, and a root from the family's vineyard in his pocket." The grandfather, who long ago moved to California's wine country, points at this particular vine and says, "This is the root I brought with me—a descendant from the root the first Pedro brought with him. All our vines come from this one." It's not just the root of the vineyard, he says. "It's the root of our lives."

Later that statement proves to be true. The girl's father discovers the deception, and in a drunken rage, he throws a lantern at the G.I. The fire spreads, and in the end, the entire vineyard—acres and acres of beautiful grape vines—is lost in the blaze. The grandfather turns to the young man and says, "The fire burned through everything. There's no root stock left to replant." The vineyard is finished.

But Reeves' character returns to the stump that now marks

the spot where that one special vine stood. He pulls up the root and brings it back to the family. The father cuts it open and finds it green and alive. Cutting off a piece, he hands it to the younger man. "This is the root of your life—the root of your family," he says. "You are bound to this land and to this family by commitment, by honor, by love. Plant it. It will grow."

That story is a parable for ministry. Circumstances change—the root doesn't. Sometimes you will celebrate new growth and abundant fruitfulness. Sometimes you will endure the harsh realities of loss. Regardless of your place on that spectrum, go back to the root—Jesus. Strip away the other stuff. Just plant Jesus into the lives of people in your congregation, in your ministry, in your community, and in the world at large. God's promise echoes in the words of that father. "Plant it. It will grow."

Sow This Book into Your Life

1. Give a good, biblical definition for abiding, but express it in language that a contemporary, unchurched person could understand.

_____

_____

_____

_____

2. What is the relationship between "abiding" and "letting God be God?"

_____

_____

_____

3. What is your patience quotient? On the scale below, circle the number that best matches your outlook.

0   1   2   3   4   5   6   7   8   9   10

I expect
immediate
results

I will wait as long
as needed and
will even rejoice

4. What does your answer reveal about your commitment to abiding?

_____

_____

_____

5. How is that reflected in your church or ministry?

_____

_____

_____

6. What steps do you need to take to get back to the root in your personal life? What about in the corporate life of your church?

_____

_____

_____

7. How has this book affected your view of spiritual harvest?

_____

_____

_____

↙ appendix

Suggested Resources for
Cross-Cultural Research

We suggest that you consider befriending and spending time with international students and/or immigrants that live near you. Most cities have some type of educational institution, which generally attracts students from other countries and cultures. Research indicates the vast majority of those students will never be invited into an American home. That is tragic for many reasons related to evangelism and missions, including the virtual waste of cultural experience that would be helpful to anyone interested in helping to grow God's global kingdom.

Publications like *National Geographic* have marvelous information about cultures from all over the world. Some broadly distributed publications like *Time* magazine have regional editions for places like Europe or Asia. Those are good places to look for cultural information.

Beyond that, here are some of the many additional resources available.

Cross-Cultural Conflict: Building Relationships for Effective Ministry, written by Duane Elmer and published by Intervarsity Press. A former missionary gives practical insight for approaching a new culture. This book is full of wonderful examples of cultural conflict and steps for resolving cultural issues.

The *Culture Shock!* series produced by the Graphic

P   A   R   A

Arts Center Publishing Company of Portland Oregon. This interesting series of guides to cultural history, insight, and customs covers more than 75 destinations. These books can give valuable insight concerning the people from a particular nationality.

Doing Business Internationally: The Workbook to Cross Cultural Success, written by Terence Brake and Danielle Walker, and published by Princeton Training Press. This book is a practical guide to identifying differences in cultures. Identifying ten distinct characteristics of culture, this workbook will teach you to classify any culture in these ten areas and use this information to overcome barriers to communication and understanding.

Neighboring Faiths: A Christian Introduction to World Religions, written by Winfried Corduan, and published by Intervarsity Press. This book is a great introduction to all of the world's major religions with an emphasis on under-standing and evangelism. Religions included are; Judaism, Islam, Zoroastrianism, African Religion, Native Americans, Hinduism, Buddhism, Chinese religion, Japanese religion, and others.

Operation World, written by Patrick Johnstone and Jason Mandryk, and published by Pasternoster Lifestyle. This daily prayer guide offers basic data and statistics about every coun-try, including information about people groups living within each country.

Perspectives on the World Christian Movement, edited by Winter and Hawthorne, and published by William Carey Library. This reader contains many articles from top missiolo-gists of our day. The section entitled "The Cultural Perspective" includes information concerning "Gospel and Culture" as well as "Culture and Communication." This resource provides excellent articles to explain the role of culture in communicating the gospel.

Reaching the World in Our Own Backyard: A Guide to Building Relationships with People of Other Faiths and Cultures, written by Rajendra Pillai, and published by Waterbrook Press. Pillai, who specializes in diversity training, offers both general principles for communicating cross-culturally and specific suggestions for relating with people from different countries.

World Mission: An Analysis of the World Christian Movement. 2nd edition. Part 3. Cross Cultural Considerations, edited by Jonathan Lewis, and published by William Carey Library. This resource explores the challenges of communicating the gospel cross-culturally. Simplifying major articles from top missions experts of our day, this resource covers practical and theoretical examples of crossing cultures for the sake of the gospel as well as strategies for success. Chapter titles included are Mission and Culture, Becoming a Belonger, Keys to Communication, Church Growth and Social Structures, World Christian teamwork.

Web Resources

Bethany Prayer Profiles, compiled by Bethany World Prayer Center, Baker, LA. Available online at http://www.ksafe.come/profiles/home.html. Over one thousand profiles and summaries of the world's least reached cultures and people groups. Some profiles are available online, but the entire set can be purchased for your reference library.

The CIA World Fact Book can be accessed at http://www.cia.gov/cia/publications/factbook. This resource gives a country-by-country outline featuring political information, data on weather and economics, as well as maps, flags, etc.

The Evangelism Toolbox, http://www.evangelism.com, provides practical evangelism articles and resources for many of the world's language groups.

———————

For additional information, please contact:

Accelerating International Mission Strategies (AIMS)
PO Box 64534
Virginia Beach, VA 23467
(757) 226-5850

Or visit our website at www.aims.org

↙ notes

Introduction

[1] Tom Telford with Lois Shaw, *Missions in the 21ˢᵗ Century: Getting Your Church into the Game* (Wheaton, IL: Harold Shaw Publishers, 1998), 61.

Chapter 1: Paradigm Lost

[1] Leonard Sweet, *Soul Tsunami: Sink or Swim in New Millennium Culture* (Grand Rapids, MI: Zondervan Publishing House, 1999), 102.

[2] Peter and Paul Lalonde, *2000 A.D. Are You Ready?* (Nashville, TN: Thomas Nelson Publishers, 1997), 9, 24.

[3] "9-in-10 School-Age Children Have Computer Access; Internet Use Pervasive, Census Bureau Reports," <http://www.census.gov/Press-Release/www/2001/cb01-147.html> (posted Sept. 6, 2001).

[4] Leonard Sweet, *Soul Tsunami*, 114.

[5] Nicholas Le Quesne, "The Grass Is Greener in France," *Time Europe*, <http://www.time.com/time/europe/magazine/2002/0422/cover/rural.html> (posted Sunday, April 14, 2002; accessed April 21, 2004).

[6] "UK Agricultural Review," from *nfuonline*, <http://www.nfu.org.uk/stellentdev/groups/public/documents/farming_facts/agriculturalrevie_ia412f45c1-1.hcsp> (accessed April 21, 2004).

[7] Wendell Berry, "Agricultural Solutions for Agricultural

Problems," in *The Gift of Good Land: Further Essays Cultural and Agricultural* (San Francisco, CA: North Point Press, 1981), 113.

[8] Ibid., 114.

[9] Leland Ryken, James C. Wilhoit, Tremper Longmann III, eds., *Dictionary of Biblical Imagery* (Downers Grove, IL: InterVarsity Press, 1998), 269.

[10] Christian A. Schwarz, *Natural Church Development: A Guide to Eight Essential Qualities of Healthy Churches,* 3rd ed. (Carol Stream, IL: Church Smart Resources, 1998), 8.

[11] Ibid., 8, 10.

[12] Ibid., 8–9.

[13] Unless otherwise noted, Hebrew terms and definitions are from James Strong, *The Exhaustive Concordance of the Bible: Together with Dictionaries of the Hebrew and Greek Words* Hebrew lexicon portion (McLean, VA: MacDonald Publishing Company, nd), 54, 66, 96, 106, 107.

[14] Winkie Pratney, *Healing the Land: A Supernatural View of Ecology* (Grand Rapids, MI: Chosen Books, 1993), 26.

[15] Ibid.

[16] Linda McNatt, "Growing grass for cash: Suffolk farmer enters state's largest sector of agriculture," *The Virginian-Pilot*, D-1, D-2 (December 8, 2000).

Chapter 2: Lord of the Land

[1] Howard-Yana Shapiro and John Harrison, *Gardening for the Future of the Earth* (New York: Bantam Books, 2000), 66.

[2] Ibid.

[3] Leonard Sweet, *Soul Tsunami* (Grand Rapids, MI: Zondervan Publishing House, 1999), 260.

[4] Alfred Edersheim, *Sketches of Jewish Social Life* (Peabody,

MA: Hendrickson Publishers, 1994), 1.

5 David C. Hopkins, *The Highlands of Canaan* (Decatur, GA: The Almond Press, Columbia Theological Seminary, 1985), 79–80, 82–85.

6 "The Environment of the Bible," in *Eerdman's Family Encyclopedia of the Bible* (Grand Rapids, MI: Wm. B. Eerdman's Publishing Co., 1978), 1–15.

7 Ralph Gower, *The New Manners and Customs of Bible Times* (Chicago, IL: Moody Press, 1987), 86–87.

8 Hopkins, *The Highlands of Canaan*, 79–80, 82–85.

9 Berry, *The Gift of Good Land*, 270.

10 Ibid., 270–272.

11 Ibid., 272.

12 Ibid., 272.

13 Pratney, *Healing the Land*, 15–16.

14 Steve Hayner, "The Joy of Tending God's Garden," *World Christian* 13, no. 4, (December 2000), 6.

Chapter 3: Lord of Time

1 Pratney, *Healing the Land*, 106.

2 Strong, *The Exhaustive Concordance of the Bible*, 112.

3 John Oswalt, *The Leisure Crisis: A Biblical Perspective on Guilt-Free Leisure* (Wheaton, IL: Victor Books, 1987), 8, 25.

4 Leonard Sweet, *Aqua Church* (Loveland, CO: Group Publishing, 1999), 152.

5 Charles F. Pfeiffer, Everett F. Harrison, eds., *The Wycliffe Bible Commentary* (Chicago, IL: Moody Press, 1962), 420.

6 Hopkins, *The Highlands of Canaan*, 207.

7 Ralph W. Harris, Stanley M. Horton, Gayle Garrity Seaver,

eds., *The New Testament Study Bible: Hebrews—Jude* (Springfield, MO: World Library Press, Inc., 1986), 53.

[8] Leland Ryken, *Redeeming the Time: A Christian Approach to Work and Leisure* (Grand Rapids, MI: Baker Books, 1995), 270.

[9] Bruce Larson, *Living Out the Book of Acts* (Dallas, TX: Word Publishing, 1984), 22–23.

[10] Ibid., 25–26.

[11] Craig Brian Larson, ed., *Illustrations for Preaching and Teaching from Leadership Journal* (Grand Rapids, MI: Baker Books, 1993), 167.

[12] Abraham Joshua Heschel, *The Sabbath* (New York: Harper Collins, 1955), 32.

[13] Ken Blue, "D-Day before V-E Day," in Ralph D. Winter and Steven C. Hawthoren, eds. *Perspectives on the World Christian Movement*, 3rd Edition (Pasadena, CA: William Carey Library, 1999), 72. Reprinted from Ken Blue, *Authority to Heal* (Downers Grove, IL: InterVarsity Press, 1979).

[14] Tony Campolo, *How to Rescue the Earth without Worshipping Nature* (Nashville, TN: Thomas Nelson Publishers, 1992), 46.

Chapter 4: The Lord of Harvest

[1] Antoinette Russell told her story on *Today*, NBC, Feb. 16, 2001.

[2] Rosen, *Christ in the Passover*, 21.

[3] Ibid., 22.

[4] Ibid., 25.

[5] Alfred Edersheim, *The Temple: Its Ministry and Services*, Updated Edition (Peabody, MA: Hendrickson Publishers, Inc., 1994), 203–205.

[6] Victor Buksbazen, *The Gospel in the Feasts of Israel* (Fort Washington, PA: Christian Literature Crusade, 1978), 16.

[7] Mitch and Zhava Glaser, *The Fall Feasts of Israel* (Chicago, IL: Moody Press, 1987), 82.

[8] Ibid., 158–159.

[9] Ibid., 168.

[10] Ibid., 210.

[11] Ben Logan, *The Land Remembers: The Story of a Farm and Its People* (New York, NY: The Viking Press, 1975), 220.

[12] Ibid., 223.

Chapter 5: What is Harvest?

[1] Dan Fouts, "Crucial Simplicity," in Jack Canfield, Mark Victor Hansen, Mark & Chrissy Donnelly, Tim Tunney, eds., *Chicken Soup for the Sports Fan's Soul* (Deerfield Beach, FL: Healthy Communications, Inc., 2000), 155–156.

[2] Logan, *The Land Remembers*, 24–26.

[3] Patrick Johnstone and Jason Mandryk, *Operation World: When We Pray God Works, 21st Century Edition* (Carlisle, UK; Pasternoster, 2001), 84.

[4] George Barna, "Profile of American Churches Shows Them to be Conservative, Evangelical, Seeker-Sensitive and Losing Ground," September 8, 1998 <http://www.barna.org/cgi-bin/PagePressRelease.asp?PressReleaseID=6&Reference=B> (accessed June 11, 2001).

[5] George Barna, "Beliefs: Salvation" <http://www.barna.org/cgi-bin/PageCategory.asp?CategoryID=4> (accessed June 11, 2001).

[6] "Tracking trends: An interview with George Barna", *Baptist Press News* <http://www.sbcbaptistpress.org/bpnews.asp?Id=17436> (posted Jan. 14, 2004).

[7] Johnstone and Mandryk, *Operation World*, 51, 55.

[8] Ibid., 659

[9] Paul Borthwick, *Six Dangerous Questions to Transform Your View of the World* (Downers Grove, IL: InterVarsity Press, 1996), 87,89.

[10] "BroccoSprouts: Nutritional Content of BroccoSprouts" Brassica Foundation for Chemoprotection Research, Inc. <http://www.broccolisprouts.com/sprouts/faq.htm> (accessed April 26, 2004).

[11] John R. W. Stott, *Basic Christianity* (London, England: InterVarsity Press, 1997), 136.

[12] Ibid., 140.

[13] James F. Engel and H. Wilbur Norton, *What's Gone Wrong with the Harvest* (Grand Rapids, MI: Zondervan Publishing House, 1975), 44–45.

[14] Ibid., 46.

[15] Ibid., 68.

[16] Logan, *The Land Remembers*, 7, 13.

Chapter 6: Clearing the Land

[1] Richard Wurmbrand, *Tortured for Christ* (Glendale, CA: Diane Books, 1967), 36–37.

[2] Brother Andrew with Susan DeVore Williams, *And God Changed His Mind . . . Because His People Dared to Ask* (Tarrytown, NY: Chosen Books, Fleming H. Revell Company, 1990), 12, 13.

[3] Andrew Murray, *With Christ in the School of Prayer*, (Springdale, PA: Whitaker House, 1981), 133–134.

[4] Ibid., 135.

[5] Ibid., 137.

[6] Derek Prince, *Shaping History Through Prayer and Fasting: How Christians Can Change World Events Through the Simple yet Powerful Tools of Prayer and Fasting* (Fort Lauderdale, FL:

Derek Prince Ministries, 1973), 105.

[7] Wesley Duewel, *Revival Fire* (Grand Rapids, MI: Zondervan Publishing House, 1995), 355.

[8] Ibid, 126, 185, 186.

[9] Luis Bush and Beverly Pegues, *The Move of the Holy Spirit in the 10/40 Window* (Seattle, WA: YWAM Publishing, 1999), 21.

[10] Ibid., 22.

Chapter 7: Preparing the Soil

[1] Alfred Edersheim, *The Life and Times of Jesus the Messiah* (Hendrickson Publishers: Peabody, MA, 1993), 404–405.

[2] William Barclay, *And Jesus Said: A Handbook on the Parables of Jesus* (Philadelphia, PA: The Westminster Press, 1970), 18.

[3] Phillip Keller, *A Gardener Looks at the Fruits of the Spirit*, in *The Inspirational Writings of Phillip Keller: Four Bestselling Works Complete in One Volume* (New York, NY: Inspirational Press, 1986), 445.

[4] Barclay, *And Jesus Said*, 19.

[5] Keller, *A Gardener*, 468.

[6] Strong, *The Exhaustive Concordance of the Bible*, 44, #2790.

[7] Patrick Johnstone, *Operation World: The Day-by-Day Guide to Praying for the World* (Grand Rapids, MI: Zondervan Publishing House, 1993), 334, 336–337.

[8] Ibid., 131.

[9] Hopkins, *The Highlands of Canaan*, 191.

[10] Ibid., 203–205, 207–208.

[11] Jim Petersen, *Evangelism as a Lifestyle: Reaching into Your World with the Gospel* (Colorado Springs, CO: NavPress, 1986), 28, 31.

[12] Ibid., 42.

[13] Ibid.

[14] George Barna, "Discipleship Insights Revealed in New Book by George Barna," November 28, 2000 <http://www.barna.org/cgi-bin/PagePressRelease.asp?PressREleaseID=76&Reference=B> (accessed June 11, 2001).

[15] Charles Colson with Ellen Santilli Vaughn, *The Body: Being Light in Darkness* (Dallas: Word Publishing, 1992), 41, 42.

[16] George Barna, "Christians Are More Likely to Experience Divorce Than are Non-Christians," December 21, 1999 <http://www.barna.org/cgi-bin/PagePressRelease.asp?PressReleaseID=39&Reference=C> (accessed June 11, 2001).

[17] Johnstone and Mandryk, *Operation World*, 53.

[18] Vinita Hampton and Carol Plueddemann, *World Shapers: A Treasury of Quotes from Great Missionaries* (Wheaton, IL: Harold Shaw Publishers, 1991), 99–100.

[19] George Barna, "Researcher Predicts Mounting Challenges to Christian Church," April 2001 <http://www.barna.org/cgi-bin/PressPageRelease.asp?PressReleaseID=88&Reference=F> (accessed June 11, 2001).

Chapter 8: Matching the Seed to the Soil

[1] US Department of Agriculture (USDA), *Agricultural Fact Book*, Office of Communications, November 1998.

[2] Strong, *The Exhaustive Concordance of the Bible*, 10, #238; 118, #8085.

[3] Ibid., 50, #3256; 52, #3384.

[4] Ibid., 74, #4941; 120, #8199.

[5] R.A. Torrey, *The Power of Prayer and the Prayer of Power* (Grand Rapids, MI: Zondervan Publishing House, 1924), 16.

[6] Anthony Livesey, *Great Commanders and Their Battles* (New York, NY: Macmillan Publishing Company, 1987), 36–43.

[7] Craig Brian Larson, ed., *Illustrations for Preaching and Teaching from Leadership Journal* (Grand Rapids, MI: Baker Books, 1993), 7.

[8] Sweet, *Aqua Church*, 40.

[9] Jim Petersen, *Evangelism for Our Generation: The Practical Way to Make Evangelism Your Lifestyle* (Colorado Springs, CO: NavPress, 1985), 17, 18.

[10] Sweet, *Soul Tsunami*, 45.

[11] Sweet, *Aqua Church*, 18.

Chapter 9: Sowing the Seed

[1] Kenny Ausubel, *Seeds of Change: The Living Treasure: The Passionate Story of the Growing Movement to Restore Biodiversity and Revolutionize the Way We Think about Food* (San Francisco: HarperCollins, 1994), 70–71.

[2] W.E. Vine, *Vine's Expository Dictionary of New Testament Words, Complete and Unabridged* (Westwood, NJ: Barbour and Company, Inc., 1952), 229–230.

[3] Sweet, *Soul Tsunami*, 88.

[4] Charles T. Cook, ed., *C.H. Spurgeon's Sermons on the Parables* (London: Marshall, Morgan and Scott, 1977), 18.

[5] Ausubel, *Seeds of Change*, 1.

[6] Barclay, *And Jesus Said*, 125.

[7] Sweet, *Aqua Church*, 29, 30.

[8] Ausubel, *Seeds of Change*, 63.

[9] Berry, *The Gift of Good Land*, 8.

[10] Carol Kaesuk Yoon (*The New York Times*), "Simple Method Found to Vastly Increase Crop Yields," *New York Times*, Aug. 22, 2000, <http://nytimes.com/learning/general/ featured_articles /000822tuesday.html> (accessed November 9, 2001).

[11] Christian A. Schwarz, *Natural Church Development: A Guide to Eight Essential Qualities of Healthy Churches* 3rd ed. (Carol Stream, IL: Church Smart Resources, 1998), 34.

[12] Shapiro and Harrison, *Gardening for the Future of the Earth*, 15.

[13] Schwarz, *Natural Church Development*, 47–48.

[14] Ibid., 45.

[15] Ibid., 48.

[16] Torrey, *The Power of Prayer and the Prayer of Power*, 36–38.

[17] Ibid., 42.

Chapter 10: Nurturing the Crop

[1] Mona Riley and Brad Sargent, *Unwanted Harvest?* (Nashville, TN: Broadman & Holman Publishers, 1995), 89.

[2] Ausubel, *Seeds of Change*, 6–7.

[3] Merrill F. Unger, *Unger's Bible Dictionary* (Chicago, IL: Moody Press, 1966), 264.

[4] Bill Hull, *The Disciplemaking Church* (Grand Rapids, MI: Fleming H. Revell, A Division of Baker Book House Co., 1990), 21.

[5] Colson *The Body: Being Light in Darkness*, 130.

[6] Riley and Sargent, *Unwanted Harvest?*, 62–63.

[7] Vine, *Vine's Expository Dictionary of New Testament Words*, 158.

[8] Riley and Sargent, *Unwanted Harvest?*, 189.

[9] Ibid., 28.

[10] Barclay, *And Jesus Said*, 38.

[11] Ibid.

[12] Ibid., 39.

[13] Ibid., 43.

[14] Joy Dawson, *Intercession, Thrilling and Fulfilling* (Seattle, WA: YWAM Publishing, 1997), 192.

[15] Cynthia Vagnetti, *The Digital Journalist*, "Gifts and Graces of the Land" <http://digitaljournalist.org/issue9907/gift09htm> (accessed November 21, 2000).

Chapter 11: Harvest

[1] Riley and Sargent, *Unwanted Harvest?*, 182–183.

[2] Robert C. Williams, *Fordson, Farmall, and Poppin' Johnny: A History of the Farm Tractor and Its Impact on America* (Urbana and Chicago: University of Illinois Press, 1987), 150.

[3] *The Rising Son Newsletter*, 2, no. 2 <http://www.thejapannet.com/prod06.htm, (accessed September 28, 2001).

[4] Williams, *Fordson, Farmall*, 3.

[5] Daniel N. Lapedes, ed., *McGraw-Hill Encyclopedia of Food, Agriculture and Nutrition* (New York, St. Louis, San Francisco: McGraw-Hill Book Company, 1977), 69.

[6] Hopkins, *The Highlands of Canaan*, 38.

[7] Williams, *Fordson, Farmall*, vii.

[8] Sweet, *Soul Tsunami*, 221.

[9] Williams, *Fordson, Farmall*, 149–150.

[10] Ausubel, *Seeds of Change*, 72.

[11] Riley and Sargent, *Unwanted Harvest?*, 174, 175.

[12] Ibid., 175.

[13] Murray, *With Christ in the School of Prayer*, 69

[14] Strong, *The Exhaustive Concordance of the Bible*, 26, #1544.

Chapter 12: After Harvest, Then What?

[1] <http://scottishculture.about.com/library/blfamwatsonwatt.htm> (accessed September 25, 2001)

[2] Larson, *Illustrations for Preaching and Teaching from Leadership Journal*, 220.

[3] Louise Eubank Gray, *A Patchwork Quilt: Life on a Virginia Farm 1910–1920* (Lawrenceville, VA: Brunswick Publishing Corporation, 1989), 20–21.

[4] Hampton and Plueddemann, *World Shapers*, 59.

[5] Charles Finney, "Lecture I—What a Revival of Religion Is," in *Revival Lectures* <http://twtministries.com/articles/12_revival/flectur/lectur01.html> (accessed Oct. 18, 2004).

[6] Ruth A. Tucker, *From Jerusalem to Irian Jaya: A Biographical History of Christian Missions* (Grand Rapids, MI: Academie Books, Zondervan Publishing House, 1983), 67.

[7] Ibid., 68.

[8] Ben Dungan, "Harvesting Seeds," from *i Can Garden,* June 16, 2001 <http://www.icangarden.com/document.cfm?task=viewdetail&itemid=2560&categoryid=42> (accessed Dec. 6, 2001).

[9] Chuck Bennett, "The Problem with Success," *Evangelical Mission Quarterly* 32, no. 1 (January, 1996): 20–26.

[10] Gayla Sanders, "Harvesting Seeds," *You Grow Girl* <http://www.yougrowgirl.com/grow/seedharvest.php> (accessed Dec. 6, 2001).

[11] "Collecting Seeds: Create your own heirloom plants by saving seeds." *Garden Gate,* <http://www.gardengatemagazine.com/basics/collectseeds.html> (accessed Dec. 6, 2001).

[12] Win Arn and Charles Arn, *The Master's Plan for Making Disciples: Every Christian an Effective Witness through an Enabling Church*, 2nd Edition (Grand Rapids, MI: Baker Book House Co., 1992, 1998), 13.

[13] "Collecting Seeds," *Garden Gate.*

[14] "Threshing Floor," <http://www.cresourcei.org/phototour/pfbw_thresh.html> (accessed Dec. 6, 2001).

[15] "Threshing," in *Farm Sermons by C. H. Spurgeon*, <http://www.spurgeon.org/misc/thresh.htm> (accessed Dec. 6, 2001).

[16] Ralph Winter, "The Kingdom Strikes Back: The Ten Epochs of Redemptive History," in *Perspectives on the World Christian Movement*, The Institute of International Studies (Pasadena, CA: The William Carey Library, 1981), 148.

[17] Watchcry Quotes: Provoking Thoughts on Prayer, Revival and Missions," <http://www.watchword.org/fire_from_the_altar_of_prayer.htm> (accessed Feb. 15, 2001).

Chapter 13: Fruit that Remains

[1] Beulah Collins, ed., *For Benefit of Clergy* (NY: Grosset & Dunlap, 1966), 95.

[2] Ralph W. Harris, MA, exec.ed., Stanley M. Horton, Th.D., ed., *The Complete Biblical Library, The New Testament Study Bible, John* (Springfield, MO: World Library Press Inc., 1991) 413, 415.

[3] Strong, *The Exhaustive Concordance of the Bible*, 47 in the Greek portion, #3306.

[4] "Fire from the Altar of Prayer," 1, <http://www.watchword.org/fire_from_the_altar_of_prayer.htm> accessed February 15, 2001.

[5] Bruce Wilkinson, *The Secrets of the Vine: Breaking Through to Abundance* (Sisters, OR: Multnomah Publishers, 2001), 55–56.

[6] Ibid., 59.

[7] Ibid., 61, 73.

[8] Selwyn Hughes, *The Introvert's Guide to Spontaneous Witnessing: How to Share Your Faith With Others Naturally and Effectively* (Minneapolis, MN: Bethany House Publishers, 1983),

118–119.

[9] Ibid., 123.

[10] Sweet, *Soul Tsunami*, 253–254.

[11] Strong, Hebrew portion, 27, #1523; 88, #5937.

[12] "Fire from the Altar of Prayer," 13.

[13] *A Walk in the Clouds*, Twentieth Century Fox, Zucker Brothers Production, 1995.

< bibliography

Andrew, Brother, with Susan DeVore Williams. *And God Changed His Mind . . . Because His People Dared to Ask.* Tarrytown, NY: Chosen Books / Fleming H. Revell Company, 1990.

Alexander, Pat, ed. *Eerdman's Family Encyclopedia of the Bible.* Grand Rapids, MI: Wm. B. Eerdman's Publishing Co., 1978.

Arn, Win, and Charles Arn. *The Master's Plan for Making Disciples: Every Christian an Effective Witness through an Enabling Church,* 2nd ed. Grand Rapids, MI: Baker Book House Co., 1998.

Ausubel, Kenny. *Seeds of Change: The Living Treasure: The Passionate Story of the Growing Movement to Restore Biodiversity and Revolutionize the Way We Think about Food.* San Francisco: HarperCollins, 1994.

Baptist Press News, "Tracking Trends: An Interview with George Barna," in *BP News*, January 6, 2004. <http://www.sbcbaptistpress.org/bpnews.asp?Id=17436>.

Barclay, William. *And Jesus Said: A Handbook on the Parables of Jesus.* Philadelphia, PA: The Westminster Press, 1970.

Barna, George. "Beliefs: Salvation," June 11, 2001. <http://www.barna.org/cgi-bin/PageCategory.asp?CategoryID=4>.

————. "Christians Are More Likely to Experience Divorce Than are Non Christians," December 21, 1999. <http://

P   A   R   A

arse
www.barna.org/cgi-bin/PagePressRelease.asp?PressReleaseI
D=39&Reference=C>

———. "Discipleship Insights Revealed in New Book by George
Barna," November 28, 2000. <http://www.barna.org/cgi-bin/
PagePressRelease.asp?PressReleaseID=76&Reference=B>.

———. "Profile of American Churches Shows Them to be
Conservative, Evangelical, Seeker-Sensitive and Losing
Ground," September 8, 1998. <http://www.barna.org/cgi-bin/
PagePressRelease.asp?PressReleaseID=6&Reference=B>.

———. "Researcher Predicts Mounting Challenges to Christian
Church," April 2001. <http://www.barna.org/cgi-bin/PressPa
geRelease.asp?PressReleaseID=88&Reference=F>,

Bennett, Chuck. "The Problem with Success," *Evangelical
Mission Quarterly* 32, no. 1 (January 1996): 20–26.

Berry, Wendell. *The Gift of Good Land: Further Essays Cultural
and Agricultural.* San Francisco: North Point Press, 1981.

Blue, Ken. *Authority to Heal*, 3rd Edition. Downers Grove, IL:
InterVarsity Press, 1999.

Borthwick, Paul. *Six Dangerous Questions to Transform Your
View of the World.* Downers Grove, IL: InterVarsity Press,
1996.

Buksbazen, Victor. *The Gospel in the Feasts of Israel.* Fort
Washington, PA: Christian Literature Crusade, 1954.

Bush, Luis, and Beverly Pegues. *The Move of the Holy Spirit in
the 10/40 Window.* Seattle, WA: YWAM Publishing, 1999.

Campolo, Tony. *How to Rescue the Earth without Worshipping
Nature.* Nashville, TN: Thomas Nelson Publishers, 1992.

Colson, Charles, with Ellen Santilli Vaughn. *The Body: Being
Light in Darkness.* Dallas: Word Publishing, 1992.

Cook, Charles T., ed., *C.H. Spurgeon's Sermons on the
Parables.* London: Marshall, Morgan & Scott, 1977.

Dawson, Joy. *Intercession, Thrilling and Fulfilling.* Seattle, WA: YWAM Publishing, 1997.

Duewel, Wesley. *Revival Fire.* Grand Rapids, MI: Zondervan Publishing House, 1995.

Dungan, Ben. "Harvesting Seeds," from *i Can Garden,* June 16, 2001. <http://www.icangarden.com/document.cfm?task=vie wdetail&itemid=2560&categoryid=42>.

Edersheim, Alfred. *The Life and Times of Jesus the Messiah.* Peabody, MA: Hendrickson Publishers, 1993.

Edersheim, Alfred. *Sketches of Jewish Social Life: Updated Version.* Peabody, MA: Hendrickson Publishers, 1994.

Edersheim, Alfred. *The Temple: Its Ministry and Services: Updated Edition.* Peabody, MA: Hendrickson Publishers, Inc., 1994.

Engel, James F., and H. Wilbur Norton. *What's Gone Wrong with the Harvest?* Grand Rapids, MI: Zondervan Publishing House, 1975.

Finney, Charles. "Lecture I—What a Revival of Religion Is," in *Revival Lectures.* <http://twtministries.com/articles/12_ revival/flectur/lectur01.html>.

Fouts, Dan. "Crucial Simplicity," in Jack Canfield, Mark Victor Hansen, Mark & Chrissy Donnelly, Tim Tunney, eds., *Chicken Soup for the Sports Fan's Soul.* Deerfield Beach, FL: Healthy Communications, Inc., 2000.

Garden Gate Magazine. "Collecting Seeds: Create your own heirloom plants by saving seeds." Dec. 6, 2001. <http://www .gardengatemagazine.com/basics/collectseeds.html>.

Glaser, Mitch and Zhava Glaser. *The Fall Feasts of Israel.* Chicago, IL: Moody Press, 1987.

Gower, Ralph, *The New Manners and Customs of Bible Times.* Chicago, IL: Moody Press, 1987.

Gray, Louise Eubank. *A Patchwork Quilt: Life on a Virginia Farm 1910–1920*. Lawrenceville, VA: Brunswick Publishing Corporation, 1989.

Hampton, Vinita and Carol Plueddemann. *World Shapers: A Treasury of Quotes from Great Missionaries*. Wheaton, IL: Harold Shaw Publishers, 1991.

Harris, Ralph W., Stanley M. Horton, Gayle Garrity Seaver, eds. *The New Testament Study Bible: Hebrews—Jude*. Springfield, MO: World Library Press, Inc., 1986.

———. *The New Testament Study Bible: John*. Springfield, MO: World Library Press Inc., 1991.

Hayner, Steve, "The Joy of Tending God's Garden," *World Christian* 13, no. 4, December 2000.

Heschel, Abraham Joshua. *The Sabbath*. New York: HarperCollins, 1951.

Hopkins, David C. *The Highlands of Canaan: Agricultural Life in the Early Iron Age*. Decatur, GA: The Almond Press, Columbia Theological Seminary, 1985.

Hughes, Selwyn . *The Introvert's Guide to Spontaneous Witnessing: How to Share Your Faith With Others Naturally and Effectively*. Minneapolis, MN: Bethany House Publishers, 1983.

Hull, Bill. *The Disciplemaking Church*. Grand Rapids, MI: Fleming H. Revell, A Division of Baker Book House Co., 1990.

Johnstone, Patrick. *Operation World: The Day-by-Day Guide to Praying for the World*. Grand Rapids, MI: Zondervan Publishing House, 1993.

Johnstone, Patrick, and Jason Mandryk. *Operation World: When We Pray God Works, 21st Century Edition*. Carlisle, UK: Pasternoster, 2001.

Keller, Phillip. *A Gardener Looks at the Fruits of the Spirit*, in *The Inspirational Writings of Phillip Keller: Four Bestselling Works Complete in One Volume*. New York, NY: Inspirational Press, 1986.

Lalonde, Peter and Paul Lalonde, *2000 A.D. Are You Ready?* Nashville, TN: Thomas Nelson Publishers, 1997.

Lapedes, Daniel N., ed., *McGraw-Hill Encyclopedia of Food, Agriculture and Nutrition*. New York, St. Louis, San Francisco: McGraw-Hill Book Company, 1977.

Larson, Craig Brian, ed., *Illustrations for Preaching and Teaching from Leadership Journal*. Grand Rapids, MI: Baker Books, 1993.

Larson, Bruce. *Living Out the Book of Acts*. Dallas, TX: Word Publishing, 1984.

Le Quesne , Nicholas, "The Grass Is Greener in France," *Time Europe*, April 14, 2002. <http://www.time.com/time/europe/magazine/2002/0422/cover/rural.html>

Logan, Ben. *The Land Remembers: The Story of a Farm and Its People*. New York, NY: The Viking Press, 1975.

McNatt, Linda. "Growing grass for cash: Suffolk farmer enters state's largest sector of agriculture," *The Virginian-Pilot*, D1-2, December 8, 2000.

Murray, Andrew. *With Christ in the School of Prayer*. Springdale, PA: Whitaker House, 1981.

Oswalt, John. *The Leisure Crisis: A Biblical Perspective on Guilt-Free Leisure*. Wheaton, IL: Victor Books, 1987.

Otis, George, Jr. and The Sentinel Group, "The Holy Spirit Around the World," *Charisma*. January 1993, 21–73.

Petersen, Jim. *Evangelism as a Lifestyle: Reaching into Your World with the Gospel*. Colorado Springs, CO: NavPress, 1980.

————. *Evangelism for Our Generation: The Practical Way to Make Evangelism Your Lifestyle.* Colorado Springs, CO: NavPress, 1985.

Pfeiffer, Charles F. and Everett F. Harrison, eds. *The Wycliffe Bible Commentary.* Chicago, IL: Moody Press, 1962.

Pratney, Winkie. *Healing the Land: A Supernatural View of Ecology.* Grand Rapids, MI: Chosen Books, 1993.

Prince, Derek. *Shaping History Through Prayer and Fasting: How Christians can change world events through the simple yet powerful tools of prayer and fasting.* Fort Lauderdale, FL: Derek Prince Ministries, 1973.

Riley, Mona, and Brad Sargent. *Unwanted Harvest?* Nashville, TN: Broadman & Holman Publishers, 1995.

Rosen, Ceil, and Moshe Rosen. *Christ in the Passover.* Chicago, IL: Moody Bible Institute, 1978.

Ryken, Leland. *Redeeming the Time: A Christian Approach to Work and Leisure.* Grand Rapids, MI: Baker Books, 1995.

Ryken, Leland, James C. Wilhoit, and Tremper Longmann III eds. *Dictionary of Biblical Imagery.* Downers Grove, IL: InterVarsity Press, 1998.

Sanders, Gayla. "Harvesting and Saving Your Seeds," *You Grow Girl.* <http://www.yougrowgirl.com/grow/seedharvest.php>.

Schwarz, Christian A., *Natural Church Development: A Guide to Eight Essential Qualities of Healthy Churches.* Carol Stream, IL: Church Smart Resources, 1996.

Shapiro, Howard-Yana, Ph.D., and John Harrison. *Gardening for the Future of the Earth.* New York, NY: Bantam Books, 2000.

Spurgeon, C.H. "Threshing," in *Farm Sermons by C. H. Spurgeon.* Dec. 6, 2001. <http://www.spurgeon.org/misc/thresh.htm>.

Stott, John R.W. *Basic Christianity.* London, England: Inter-Varsity Press, 1958.

Strong, James, S.T.D., LL.D. *The Exhaustive Concordance of the Bible: Together with Dictionaries of the Hebrew and Greek Words.* McLean, VA: MacDonald Publishing Company, nd.

Sweet, Leonard. *Aqua Church.* Loveland, CO: Group Publishing, 1999.

———. *Soul Tsunami: Sink or Swim in New Millennium Culture.* Grand Rapids, MI: Zondervan Publishing House, 1999.

Telford, Tom with Lois Shaw, *Missions in the 21*st *Century: Getting Your Church into the Game.* Wheaton, IL: Harold Shaw Publishers, 1998.

Torrey, R.A. *The Power of Prayer and the Prayer of Power.* Grand Rapids, MI: Zondervan Publishing House, 1955.

Tucker, Ruth A. *From Jerusalem to Irian Jaya: A Biographical History of Christian Missions.* Grand Rapids, MI: Academie Books, Zondervan Publishing House, 1983.

"UK Agricultural Review," *nfuonline*, NFU for Farmers and Growers in England and Wales. <http://www.nfu.org.uk/stellentdev/groups/public/documents/farming_facts/agriculturalrevie_ia412f45c1-1.hcsp>.

Unger, Merrill. *Unger's Bible Dictionary.* Chicago, IL: Moody Press, 1957.

U.S. Census Office. *United States Department of Commerce News.* "9-in-10 school-age Children Have Computer Access; Internet Use Pervasive," September 6, 2001. <http://www.census.gov/Press-Release/www.2001/cb01-147/html>.

U.S. Department of Agriculture (USDA), Office of Communications. *Agricultural Fact Book.* November 1998.

Vagnetti, Cynthia. "Gifts and Graces of the Land," *The Digital Journalist.* <http://digitaljournalist.org/issue9907/gift09.htm>.

Vine, W.E. *Vine's Expository Dictionary of New Testament Words, Complete and Unabridged.* Westwood, NJ: Barbour and Company, Inc., 1940.

Wilkinson, Bruce. *The Secrets of the Vine: Breaking Through to Abundance.* Sisters, OR: Multnomah Publishers, 2001.

Williams, Robert C. *Fordson, Farmall, and Poppin' Johnny: A History of the Farm Tractor and Its Impact on America.* Urbana and Chicago: University of Illinois Press, 1987.

Winter, Ralph, ed. "The Kingdom Strikes Back: The Ten Epochs of Redemptive History," in *Perspectives on the World Christian Movement.* The Institute of International Studies. Pasadena, CA: The William Carey Library, 1981.

Wurmbrand, Richard. *Tortured for Christ.* Glendale, CA: Diane Books, 1967.

Yoon, Carol Kaesuk. "Simple Method Found to Vastly Increase Crop Yields," *New York Times* August 22, 2000. <http://nytimes.com/learning/general/featured_articles/000822tuesday.html>.

D   I   G   M
LOST

Other books available from
Authentic Media . . .

**Authentic
MEDIA**

129 Mobilization Drive
Waynesboro, GA 30830

For a complete catalog of Authentic publications,
please contact us at:

1-8MORE-BOOKS
ordersusa@stl.org

Cat and Dog Theology
Rethinking Our Relationship with Our Master

Bob Sjogren & Dr. Gerald Robison

There is a joke about cats and dogs that conveys their differences perfectly.

A dog says, "You pet me, you feed me, you shelter me, you love me, you must be God."
A cat says, "You pet me, you feed me, you shelter me, you love me, I must be God."

These God-given traits of cats ("You exist to serve me") and dogs ("I exist to serve you") are often similar to the theological attitudes we have in our view of God and our relationship to Him. Using the differences between cats and dogs in a light-handed manner, the authors compel us to challenge our thinking in deep and profound ways. As you are drawn toward God and the desire to reflect His glory in your life, you will worship, view missions, and pray in a whole new way. This life-changing book will give you a new perspective and vision for God as you delight in the God who delights in you.

1-884543-17-0   206 Pages

Back to Jerusalem
Three Chinese House Church Leaders Share Their Vision to Complete the Great Commission

with Paul Hattaway

Napoleon once said: "When China is moved it will change the face of the globe." Today those words are becoming a reality through the powerful spiritual vision of the Chinese church to send 100,000 missionaries across China's borders to complete the Great Commission, even in this generation!

Here Brother Yun, Peter Xu Yongze and Enoch Wang, three Chinese house church leaders who between them have spent more than 40 years in prison for their faith, explain the history and present-day reality of the Back to Jerusalem movement. Christians everywhere who are called to fulfill the Great Commission, will be thrilled by this testimony and inspired to live bolder lives as disciples of Jesus Christ today.

1-884543-89-8   176 Pages

Power of Generosity
How to Transform Yourself and Your World

David Toycen

An intimate journey down the road of giving, *The Power of Generosity* will strike a chord with all who want to fulfill a vital part of their humanity—the need to give.

Dave Toycen, President and CEO of World Vision Canada, believes generosity can save lives—both the benefactor's and the recipient's. The act of giving without an ulterior motive inherently nurtures a need human's have for significance. During three decades of traveling to the poorest and most desperate countries, Dave has seen and met individuals who have been freed by acts of generosity.

What is generosity? What motivates a person toward benevolence? *The Power of Generosity* is a practical guide to developing a spirit of generosity, providing thoughtful answers and encouragement for all those looking for ways to be more giving in their lives.

1-932805-10-9

The Skeptics Guide to the Global AIDS Crisis
Tough Questions, Direct Answers

Dale Hanson Bourke

AIDS is the biggest public health problem the world has ever faced. Yet with all the available information, many of us know little about it. There are thousands of books, websites, and professional documents about AIDS, but it takes time to search them to find the simple facts and information that dispel the myths about this pandemic.

Motivated by the obvious need for a manageable tool, Dale Hanson Bourke has compiled the essential information in a simple and straightforward way, explaining medical and political issues in everyday language. Sample questions include:

- In the United States, everyone panicked when AIDS was first reported, but now things don't seem so bad. Isn't it possible that we are overstating the problem?

- What about charities? Aren't many of them concentrating on fighting AIDS?

- How is HIV/AIDS spread in different parts of the world?

- Do condoms really stop the transmission of sexually transmitted diseases?

About the Authors

Dr. Howard Foltz is the founder and president of AIMS, Accelerating International Mission Strategies. He is also Professor of Global Evangelization at Regent University in Virginia Beach, Virginia with over 40 years of practical ministry experience. He speaks regularly in churches and at conferences throughout the United States and the world, has appeared on the 700 Club, and is a member of several boards. He is the author of several books and is training a network of people to present AIMS seminars and books.

Ruth Ford earned degrees at Asbury College in Wilmore, Kentucky and Regent University in Virginia Beach, Virginia. She worked for several years with Dr. Foltz at AIMS, Accelerating International Mission Strategies, editing publications and helping him write four books. She has worked as a freelancer on several other projects, including books, articles, and curriculum.